DIARIES OF A PARANORMALIST

Encounters with Death

GREG LAWSON

ILLUSTRATIONS BY ROB STOLT

Visionary Living Publishing/Visionary Living, Inc.
New Milford, Connecticut

Cover and interiors designed by John Cheek

ISBN: 978-1-942157-98-4 (pbk)
ISBN: 978-1-942157-99-1 (epub)

Published by Visionary Living Publishing/Visionary Living, Inc.
New Milford, Connecticut
www.visionarylivingpublishing.com

DEDICATION

For Rosemary Ellen Guiley - Pathfinder

DIARIES OF A PARANORMALIST

ACKNOWLEDGEMENTS

If it were not for the World War II veterans that congregated in the early morning hours at McVoy's Grocery in Rockdale, Texas, and shared their stories with an impressionable young man, this book would have never been written. Also, I would like to express my deepest appreciation to Rosemary Ellen Guiley for being a true inspiration and encouraging my journey into the dark. Finally, to Joy Pottinger Baun, for sacrificing her time to keep me factual, legible, and on track.

DIARIES OF A PARANORMALIST

CONTENTS

INTRODUCTION

THE LESSON

I LEARNED FROM A PARENT, a brother, and a long-eared dog. I learned from a sound, another child, and from Santa Claus; from my faults, my anger, my thirst; from my grandmother, her house, from her soft, wrinkled hand. I learned watching violence, to throw a stick, and to fetch. I learned to tie a shoe, of modesty, and when and where to look. I learned from a turtle, some slippery moss, and respect for the height of a smooth skinned tree. I learned fear from the death of a friend, the mystery of dark places, from which almost nothing good can be. I learned of pain, from cuts, bumps, and stitches; blood. I learned of compassion from a stray cat, an invalid old man, and a victim. I learned of pubescent anger, testosterone, and how destruction felt good; taking life felt good. I learned to have a secret, to keep a secret, and to tell a secret. I learned to hide, to sneak, to lie; and yes, I learned of other special things too.

I learned my grandfather died before I was born; my father would only throw ball with me once; that my mother was an adventurer. I learned that giving someone something felt good but getting something for nothing felt better; that magic existed—then didn't exist. I learned of my own flesh. I learned how to hook a worm; that slingshots can put your eye out, and certain things can cause hair growth on your chest, face, and sometimes hands. I learned my face wouldn't stick that way; puppets had masters; John Wayne was an actor.

I learned nothing worth having is free, there is satisfaction in a job well done, and everything has a price, even friendship. I learned that sometimes I would like to be a part of the problem instead of part of the solution. I learned you may have been a soldier, a sailor, an airman, or marine, and all it takes is one day to be a former of the four.

I learned from betrayal, from lust, and greed. I learned from self-service, from an old, lonely woman, and from teamwork. I learned I hadn't watched a sunrise in twenty years or seen a sunset in ten. I learned I could eat cooked meat, raw meat, frozen meat, and live meat. I learned from the clock's hands how slow time winds, how there is not enough of it in a day, and how it slips away as my hair adds gray.

I learned I'm not invincible, that pure luck has allowed me to live, and I am so, so fortunate. I learned my mother is a wondrous person—that things are not that important, and that art is. I learned families and relationships are the only things that truly last; I am still impatient and enjoy spending time alone. I learned my sister is the toughest person I know; that to finish something means I have to start it first, and paying off credit cards is rewarding, so you can charge more.

I learned that flexibility is strength and rigidity is weakness, that evolution happens, and history is not appreciated. I learned if you have two great friends in a lifetime, you're fortunate; three, you are blessed; and four, you're lying.

I learned from a woman in white, from crybaby bridge, from an abandoned old church and cemetery. I learned the world is a small place; there are strange faces everywhere, and even stranger stories.

These are some of mine.

There are hundreds of cemeteries throughout Central Texas, and they all have stories to tell.

FOREWORD

In the Beginning
Fiskville Cemetery, Austin, Texas, circa 1969

ON A BLEAK DAY IN THE FALL OF 1969, I stood staring at a tombstone. This was no ordinary tombstone—it was the tombstone of a child. My brother Bill, who was seventeen, had put me on his motorcycle and we had driven the back roads in search of graveyards. At five years old, it was not something I would have chosen to do; however, spending any time with my older brother and on his motorcycle was glorious. His mission in life was to be a good big brother and to scare me. He usually did a decent job. Whether it was taking me around to cemeteries looking for the child's grave that was closest to my age, sneaking into my room at night to make weird noises, rock climbing or skydiving, he usually succeeded.

On this particular day we had stumbled on Fiskville Cemetery by accident. It is one of Austin, Texas' oldest Anglo cemeteries with graves dating back to the 1840s. Fiskville was a little community north of Austin's Colony, which was issuing land grants from Mexico starting around 1821. While there are some Mexican and Spanish graves that are much older scattered around the area, these early ones date from the initial white occupation.

Bill and I had walked most of the graveyard marking off many of the children: 13-year-old Willie Mangan, stillborn Paul Barfield, infant boy Holt in 1942, the Sterling baby, and the closest to my age, Marvin Pittsford, aged 6 years. We stayed at Marvin's grave for a while and Bill, I am sure, told me some fantastic tale of how Marvin died and how dangerous it was to be a six-year-old. I can't clearly remember. But I am sure I said a little prayer for Marvin and probably spoke directly to him expressing that I was sorry he had died.

That was the beginning of my fascination with death and my exploration into the unknown and mysterious realms of religion, metaphysical experience, and the paranormal. Throughout elementary school, junior high, and high school, I continued seeking out and exploring cemeteries, abandoned buildings, and Indian sacred sites. I passed on the fascination to my friends by dragging them along. We explored ancient silver mines along Walnut Creek, old abandoned pioneer farms and ranches, natural caves where Indians lived and died, and occasionally found solitary family graves on lands where we trespassed. While I thought I was not interested in history, in doing the things I did, that is precisely what I was researching.

I am quite sure these experiences somehow steered me toward my vocation in law enforcement. Not only did I search for the dead as a child's hobby, my evolution culminated into specializing in suicide mediation, hostage negotiation, and homicide investigation. Today I work as the sergeant for a lake patrol unit and dive team specializing in aquatic death investigation. It seems I search for the dead as a hobby and an occupation.

One day, I will write a book about the criminal cases I have investigated and other noteworthy incidents. But for now, within these pages, I will concentrate on the formative experiences I have had involving specific places I have explored and the things I have seen.

Hope you enjoy the journey.

THE WHITE LADY
OF KINSALE

CHARLES FORT
County of Cork, Ireland, circa 2015

NEAR THE RIVER BANDON in the County of Cork, is the town of Kinsale, Ireland. Reaching out toward Kinsale Harbor is a beautiful spit of land now holding the remains of a 17th century fort known as Charles Fort. Built by the English, it was a formidable, star-shaped structure designed to ensure the English maintained rule over their Irish counterparts. Now, as they did then, the Irish did not care to be ruled by Englishmen, so much that clans actually allied with the Spanish to keep the Britons out. This of course, didn't go so well for either the Irish or the Spanish, and ultimately English soldiers were garrisoned at Charles Fort to maintain control in the region.

My visit to Charles Fort was not long; however, maybe because I am a former military man or have a reverence for battlegrounds, my experience there impacted me. While the fort itself has a lengthy and formidable past, housing political prisoners and being the location of several battles, it now serves as a reminder of what Britain once was. But maybe more, of what love once was. You see, there was a commander at Charles Fort, a Colonel Warrender. Appointed as the fort's commanding officer and governor, and under threat of immanent attack, Warrender was a staunch tactician and severe disciplinarian. He personally ensured all his officers and men adhered to exacting protocol both on and off duty. But he was also the father to a beautiful young girl whom he had raised right there in Kinsale. Her name was Wilful, a popular name at the time, and she had fallen in love with one of the English officers garrisoned there, a Sir Trevor Ashurst. Tall and handsome, Ashurst was a distinguished soldier and the son of a fine family. After the insistence of a formal courtship, the two young lovers were betrothed to be married and all was well—both Trevor and Wilful were never happier.

As you can imagine, an affair such as this, the colonel's daughter marrying an English officer, fueled excitement within the fort and the town of Kinsale. It was the grandest event of the year, possibly ever, at Charles Fort. Pomp and circumstance were the order of the day and in the custom of both the English and the Irish there were endless formalities as the dignitaries and guests arrived at the sprawling fortification. Soldiers relieved of their duties mingled with the residents, mainly the young women, as the people of Kinsale flooded through the open gates gleefully taking in their surroundings. Both a military band and a local group of minstrels entertained the crowds throughout the afternoon and there were never-ending toasts to the beautiful bride and her groom. Soon the attendees were seated, and a local priest performed the ceremony. With no conflicts or condemnations, the ritual was concluded with the priest presenting to the congregation, Mr. and Mrs. Trevor Ashurst. With the crowd on their feet, Trevor and Wilful had to fight their way back down the aisle through the throng of these laughing and backslapping well-wishers, both English and Irish alike.

After a brief adjournment, the bride and her groom joined the revelers in the main hall where they feasted and drank, accepting tributes and toasts with open arms and full glasses. They danced and hugged and made promises to old friends and new. They looked into each other's eyes while dancing or when across the room, and they saw their future. They saw their happiness. Everyone did. That afternoon would be forever in their minds, because they lived a lifetime in those few hours.

With evening approaching, Trevor and Wilful took their leave of the congregation. They said their goodbyes to the nobility that had graced the affair. They hugged and kissed their family and friends. They accepted compliments from the servants and soldiers, then arm in arm they strolled along the protective walls of Charles Fort toward the farthest lookout position, with their final intention in mind, the bridal suite.

As they reached the point, they stood staring south across the bay. On the far side, the last of the sun's rays reflected off the green rolling hills, shimmered off the blue-silver tipped waves, and shone gold on the limestone ramparts and guard turrets looming far above the rocky shore of this cold and formidable sea. There, alone and along the outside wall, Wilful saw a spray of beautiful blue flowers clinging to life.

Trevor saw them too, although his vision was somewhat impaired from the day's festivities. It was at that moment he realized Wilful had no bouquet. His bride, his beautiful Irish flower had no bouquet. Immediately, he exclaimed he would retrieve it for her. Stepping over a cannon emplacement he reached from the wall, but slipped, almost falling onto the rocks many feet below. Wilful, laughing and grabbing onto the back of his coat, held at bay her young gentleman as he leaned across the battlements.

A sentry standing guard at his turret saw Trevor's attempt and instantly offered his assistance to the newlyweds. He was aware that Trevor was too intoxicated to make a perilous climb down to the flowers and offered to do it for him, if Trevor would only stand his watch while he was at the task. The couple gladly accepted. Trevor took the man's musket and watch coat and Wilful observed intently as the soldier ran down toward the front gates to locate a length of rope to descend to the flowers. Several minutes went by.

Then half an hour.

The couple couldn't understand why the man had not returned and it was impossible for Trevor to inquire, since he could not leave his post without being properly relieved. As the sun sank and darkness cloaked the fort, Trevor kissed his wife and sent her on to the bridal suite. Meanwhile he stood his watch, waiting for the soldier to return or at the very least, for someone to relieve him. While he could have very easily called out to another soldier standing watch for liberation, he did not wish to get the young soldier in trouble for not returning. Even though he was a commissioned officer, he did not dare call out in order to avoid any confrontations with the sergeant of the guard.

There was only one real problem with this idea; it was that this was Trevor's wedding day. A wedding day filled with not only festivities, but with too much wine as well. And as the wine grappled within him, Trevor decided to sit down in the sentry turret. Soon, after leaning on his benefactor's firearm, he was asleep.

On the other side of the fort, cinching on his pistol belt, Colonel Warrender prepared for his nightly perimeter sentry inspection. Closing his logbook and securing the door to his office, he began walking the fortress's perimeter battlements, expecting the customary sentry challenge of "Who goes there?" from each post and turret. All was well until he approached the turret overlooking the point. Here, he did not receive the challenge. The colonel stepped closer and clicked his boot heels on the cobblestones as a warning to the lookout. But still, no response. Losing his patience, the colonel stepped to the narrow turret entry. There, shimmering moonlight glinted off a pristine and well-oiled musket barrel. The glow illuminated the slumped form of a man asleep on watch.

At that time, Colonel Warrender did what any commanding officer would have done catching a sentry asleep at his post. He withdrew his revolver and shot the man, then and there, through the heart. Mortally struck, the man's body simply rolled forward and onto the ground, dead, with the musket clattering at his side. The colonel yelled for the sergeant of the guard, who quickly responded with a picket of men bearing torches. After hearing the gunfire, others joined them as well. One of the soldiers was ordered to take the place of the dead man and the others were instructed to take the body to the courtyard for display in accordance with the protocol for summary executions. It was then, as they rolled him over, that Colonel Warrender saw Trevor's face. And it was then that behind him he heard his daughter's voice asking what had happened—where was Trevor?

He did not move; he could not face his daughter.

Often in such confusion, time seems to slow. Things that normally go unnoticed are clearly apparent. Sight is acute. Sounds are crystal clear. It was at this time the world was witness to this young girl's heart as it was crushed from her body, driving out a wail of terror and pain, unrepeatable.

A solitary shadow moved between the men; the outline of her shawl silhouetted by the many torchlights. It was Wilful. She briefly hesitated, then grasped her husband's lifeless form. In a moment she was at the wall, blood on her hands and bosom. The men heard the sea breeze catch and flutter in her thin bridal gown as she cleared the wall and with that final step, joined her groom in death.

Colonel Warrender, the governor of Charles Fort, County of Cork, town of Kinsale, returned to his office. He sat at his desk and made his last journal entry: *I have been relieved.*

It was there, with his revolver, he shot himself.

When I visited Charles Fort, it was this tragic tale that particularly struck me. The story's skeleton provides the structure for the legend of The White Lady of Kinsale. You will hear differing versions of the story depending on whom you ask. And the variety is just as diverse as the versions of the hauntings you will be told.

There are dozens of "White Lady" legends throughout the world. The White Lady in the Lake at Durand Eastman Park, Rochester, New York wandering about looking for the body of her daughter. The White Lady of Portchester Castle, seen retracing her steps trying to retrieve her fallen child. And the White Lady of the Berliner Schloss (Berlin Palace), possibly Countess Kunigunda of Orlamünde, who was tormented by the fact that she had murdered her young children in order to marry Albrecht of Nuremberg. These and many more lead people across the world to report such "White Lady" experiences.

As a lifelong military man and law enforcement official, I provided the above rendition of the story that made the most sense to me, based on the common theme of the many accounts, military protocol, and the particulars of the location. In some forms of the story the flowers were reported as white. I, however, saw only blue Spring Squill growing on the battlements during my visit and they are the most common flowers to grow in dry, rocky coastal areas of Ireland. In some versions, the colonel is the one that issued the challenge to the sentry; however, this is not proper military protocol. The sentry should be aware enough to detect an approaching person and issue the challenge first. In another account, Wilful awakens during the night only to find that Trevor had been shot dead and that her father had thrown himself over the wall. In her

A newly wedded bride is said to roam Charles Fort in search of
soldiers falling asleep while on guard duty.

distress, she then casts herself over the wall. However, I do not believe Wilful would have fallen asleep before Trevor returned to their bridal suite, but that could just be the romantic bias in me talking... Also, the cowardly action of the colonel killing himself before Wilful takes her own life does not sit well with the description of this career officer and strict disciplinarian. In my personal opinion...

In one account written in *The World Wide Magazine*, the colonel's surname was reported as Browne and that he shot his son, not his new son-in-law. In the book *True Irish Ghost Stories,* by St. John Seymour and Harry Neligan, they tell of possibly the first sighting of the White Lady in 1815 by a garrison officer. Described as a woman in her wedding dress, the vision disappeared when the officer tried to get a closer look.

And still, even the explanations for the hauntings vary in type and location. In some hauntings, the entity assumed to be Wilful is a wraith intent on punishing any officers for the death of her groom. In others, she is a caring ghost in her flowing wedding dress protecting the soldiers from falling asleep on duty. But in any of these stories, three facts remain true: (1) Trevor is shot and killed, (2) Wilful commits suicide, and (3) Colonel Warrender commits suicide. These are the constants.

I believe it was the turret at the southmost point that

was the location of this heartbreak. I watched as a solitary gull rode the sea breeze in front of the empty battlement and swooped now and again in front as if to confirm the post was abandoned. I stood there as long as I could, trying to make sense of it all, before I was forced to move on. That seems to be the real theme for any human endeavor, to create a sense of logic and clarity of purpose. For in this life, it is proper and correct that we should lose—everything.

That is what happens.

In all of this, it is my belief that these three souls pass on wisdom for all who care to listen. The themes of that wisdom seem to suggest you should not be hasty in making your decisions, be soundly responsible for the actions you take, and make every moment in your life count.

Every moment.

DIARIES OF A PARANORMALIST

CHERRY BLAST

FORT RICHARDSON
Alaska, circa 1984

IT SEEMS THERE IS A RITUAL, planned or not, that takes place whenever a new person joins a group or organization. An initiation of sorts. In some cases, that initiation can take the form of reciting a promise of allegiance, it can be an act of courage such as jumping from a bridge into the water, some sort of act of social defiance, or it can be an immersion in the knowledge of a legend or some secret thing. When I arrived in Alaska and was assigned as a paratrooper to the airborne unit stationed there, I was in for multiple initiations.

On my first night, I sat on my bunk reflecting on my choice of joining the Army and over my fate in being sent to Alaska—I had put Italy, Hawaii, and Panama on my dream sheet. That apparently wasn't the plan—Alaska was. Somewhere, down the hallway, I could hear footsteps.

Multiple footsteps. Getting closer. Stopping outside my barracks room door, then knocking.

"Hey, cherry, get your ass out here!"

Cherry, that would be me. I opened the door.

Seven guys from my assigned squad were there to greet me. One handed me a Budweiser and said, "Get your low-quarters, cherry. Meet us out front."

They all turned and headed toward the front barracks entrance.

I did what I was told. I went to my locker, got my dress shoes, the "low-quarters" they asked for, left my room and joined them in front of the building.

It was quiet, and the sky was ink. I could barely make out their faces.

"Get in the pit, cherry."

I looked at the platform just to the right of the front doors. A stand made from two-by-fours to practice parachute-landing falls (PLFs) onto a pit of sand. Before every jump, everyone in the unit would take turns stepping up onto the platform and jumping off, landing in the sand first with your feet, second with your calf, third with your thigh, forth with your buttocks, and fifth with your push-up muscle also known as your lats. The five points of contact for a proper parachute landing fall.

One of the guys threw me an entrenching tool. "Dig," he said.

I tried to catch the small shovel, but with the darkness, a beer in one hand and pair of shoes in the other, I just fumbled and the shovel landed in the sand.

"Dig, cherry!" a couple of the others repeated. Then all of them. "Dig, cherry!"

I sat my shoes and beer down and began digging.

"Faster, cherry! Dig like your life depends on it!"

I heard beer tabs popping.

I dug as they shouted their encouragement. I dug and dug. One foot deep then two. Two feet deep, then three. I dug until I almost got an attitude, and that is when it happened. I hit something. Harder than sand, softer than rock. I dug some more then pulled it out. It was an Army dress shoe. A burnt, mangled, low-quarter shoe.

"Stand up, cherry!"

I did.

My squad leader, Sergeant Perry, stepped up. "Your life ends today."

I was breathing hard and looking into the pit.

"Pay attention, cherry!" someone yelled.

I looked up. Someone had a flashlight and was illuminating two pieces of plywood attached to the side of the PLF platform. They were shaped in the form of grave headstones and had names on them. A black Sharpie pen landed in the sand in front of the grave markers.

"Add your name to the list, cherry," Sergeant Perry ordered.

I did as I was told.

Perry went on, "Add your name to the dead, cherry. Because we are all already dead. Do you understand?"

I didn't. I began scribbling my name. The way all the other cherries had scribbled theirs.

"Do you understand?"

"Yes, Sergeant."

Everyone broke out into laughter.

Perry looked down at me. "Cherry, you don't understand shit."

Someone screamed, "Yeeeaaah!"

He squatted down, face-to-face with me. Quietly he said, "There are men, good men, right there." He tapped the grave marker. "Right here." He tapped a name. "That is dead. And here, and here, and here. Dead, dead, dead."

I tried to comprehend.

He stood back up. "Throw your shoes in."

I went to stand up and someone forced me back down by my shoulder.

"Stay on your knees, cherry."

I threw in my shoes.

"From this point forward, you swear to never again don a pair of low-quarters! You will forever wear the boots of a paratrooper. Do you understand?"

"Roger that," I said.

"Roger that, my ass! Do you understand?" he yelled.

"I understand," I said.

"You cannot enter these halls if you have weakness in your heart!" Sergeant Perry added.

Someone poured whisky onto my shoes and they were ablaze in seconds. Someone handed me the bottle and I took a drink then passed it back.

There was laughter and jeering as I knelt there and watched my shoes burn. Like all the others.

Once the flames went down, all the men gathered there started kicking in the sand. Covering my shoes, my shame. Because that is what low-quarters represent to a paratrooper: shame.

The group of us loaded into two trucks and they drove me, chugging liquor all the way, out to Malamute drop zone about five miles from the company area. The drop zone I would eventually intimately know over the next two years. The drop zone I landed on thirty-two times under a billowing parachute without a scratch.

We got out and stood on the perimeter road, staring across the expanse of it.

The night was pitch black with no moon, only the stars. The shadows across the cleared field gave an outline of the far side. Gnarled roots and tree limbs reached up from piles scattered randomly, exactly where the bulldozers had left them when they cleared the forest years ago.

"They are here. Do you see them?" Perry asked.

I looked.

The other soldiers stared and became quiet.

"Do you see them? One landed over there." He pointed into the darkness. "Parachute static line tangled around his neck—snap! And one over there, impaled in those trees."

I did. In the shadows, I could see a soldier hunched painfully with a large pack on his back. From one of the piles I could see another reaching up to the sky as if pleading for help. Still another I could see, silent and unmoving as he stared back at me.

"They are all here. Look at them."

They were, and I saw.

Slowly, everyone turned and headed back to the trucks. I followed.

Getting in, Perry looked back at me. "Not you. You walk with them. And when you get back, know what it means to walk through those unit doors."

And eventually I did.

Over a year after my walk, I found myself once again at Malamute drop zone. This time, I was 800 feet above and struggling to look back over my head and check to see if my parachute had deployed. The cold, one-hundred-mile-an-hour air sliced at my cheeks, and the nylon harness squeezed my legs and threatened to squeeze other things. My body, suspension lines, and chute were still horizontal with the ground, because I had not slowed down enough for my weight to swing underneath the inflating fabric. Only three seconds earlier, I had been in the warm, comfortable confines of an Air Force C-130 cargo plane, flying over the frozen forest of this Alaskan drop zone. On the last number of my count to four, my stiffened body swung under the newly created nylon mushroom above. I saw my canopy was full; I had no suspension line twists, adequate height to adjust my leg straps, and then release my combat equipment on a lowering line. Everything seemed to be fine. It was four o'clock in the morning, and the sun wouldn't be up until around ten. When they say Alaskan nights are long, they mean it. This time of the year, January, we were lucky to get a good four hours of daylight. Strangely enough, though, the contrast of the snow against trees and shadows gave the panorama a look of twilight. I took a moment to soak it in. The sight was breathtaking.

Malamute drop zone carved out its picturesque surroundings for airborne training by the United States Army. Of the rolling hills surrounding it, and the mountains beyond, it etched out a scar on the land 200 yards wide and 500 yards long. Of the trees that once stood, only sheared roots violated by the bulldozer's claws remained. I saw the familiar piles of logs, once belonging to the stumps, scattered like mass graves at the beginning of the drop zone. At the time, I didn't think much about it; just that everything was cold, white, and dead. The roar of the aircraft's turbojets had receded into a faint muffle, and for a moment everything seemed quiet. The wind ruffled the leading edge of my parachute, and I saw my fellow platoon members floating all around me. They scattered in the sky as black dots against the cloud-covered ceiling. And they too silently took in the same sights and sounds as I. It was hard to believe; I was suspended under a parachute above the Alaskan wilderness.

I noticed I was drifting to my left and was about to land. I actually should say, crash. That's all a military parachute operation is, a controlled collision. If you do it right, you'll live to see another. I had done it right twenty-two times before. I reached over to my right-front suspension line riser, clamped onto it, and pulled it to my chest. This slowed my drifting to a manageable impact and I lawn-darted into the snow. Seven feet of snow. I tried to do a proper parachute-landing fall, but the snow prevented any lateral movements; I simply accordioned into the ground. I had successfully put twenty-three jumps under my belt. All of this happened in less time than it took you to read it.

As I started the search for my rucksack, I thought about how far I had come in the past year. My first combat equipment jump, after the five student jumps required at airborne school; sheer terror. I felt much more relaxed and

Malamute Drop zone in Alaska is known to soldiers as a sacred and haunted place. Paratroopers have lost their lives here in the service of their country.

confident now. However, I was not confident I was going to get out of this hole if I didn't find my snowshoes. I pulled on my lowering line, which was now leading up and out of my hole, and slowly dragged my attached equipment down in with me. I was happy to see all of it was still there. It's commonplace to have the wind tear apart your equipment on exiting the aircraft. The propeller driven turbojet of the C-130 was a little more forgiving than the blast of the so-called Cadillac of the Airborne, the jet powered C-141. I wiggled out of my harness and pushed some of the snow aside to make room for fitting my snowshoes. The shoes went on unusually easy and I climbed out of my hole. I saw my other platoon members doing the same things; gathering their rucks, S-folding the chutes in kit bags, and heading toward the assembly point on the far side of the clearing.

An 80-pound rucksack and 64 pounds of parachute make for an interesting logistical challenge for all participants involved, especially when sporting snowshoes and negotiating seven feet of fresh powder. It took the platoon over an hour to move to the assembly point, about 150 yards away.

The men gathered near a small frozen road leading into the forest. Two duce and a half trucks were hidden in the wood line to gather our parachutes. When I saw them, I was ambivalent. They were always there when we had an airborne exercise—just to collect the chutes. On my first jump, I thought our caring, kind-hearted sergeants and officers had arranged transportation for us back to the fort. I thought this for sure, because there was no way we would be able to hump these 80-pound rucksacks through ass-deep snow, all the way back to our barracks. And I was right, we didn't have to hump these 80-pound rucksacks through ass-deep snow all the way back to our barracks. We had to hump them down the road, through the woods, over some hills, across the Alaskan Range mountain pass, over two rivers and then to our barracks. Three days later. So, as I said, when I saw the trucks, I was ambivalent.

Most of us gathered in along the wood line beside the trucks and sat down on our rucks. Our rucks were the only things to separate our asses from the snow. Some of the soldiers sat and stared. Some broke out snacks to nibble on since we hadn't eaten breakfast. Some circled up to complain.

I watched the wood line. I looked for the shadow soldiers Perry had shown me.

Only a few minutes passed by and Sergeant Perry walked over. "Squad Leaders, give me a head count."

First squad leader, Sergeant Fullingcamp barked, "First squad all present!"

"Second squad present," Sergeant Peterson said.

"Third squad all present," their Sergeant said. I don't remember his name.

Then fourth squad, the weapons squad Sergeant standing over by the trucks shouted, "All up but the cherry."

Everyone chuckled. Every one of us knew what it was like to be the cherry. That is what they call you until you make your first combat equipment jump from only 800 feet. A cherry. And on your first cherry blast, your first jump, you have no idea what to expect. All you know is everyone hassles you. "Hey, cherry, go get the C-rats." "Hey, cherry, go get the artillery batteries." "Hey, cherry, go to the radio shop and get some squelch grease." "Hey, cherry, go to supply and get your canopy lights." None of these things exist. But you, the cherry, don't know that, and you run around all morning like an idiot...

And you are. I was.

I had forgotten we had a cherry on this jump. He had reported to the platoon on Friday, spent the weekend getting ready for the field, and joined us this Monday morning. I found out later, he was four months out of high school and just finished supply specialist training.

Sergeant Perry hollered to everyone, "Ya'll seen the cherry?"

No one spoke up.

"Jesus Christ, did anyone see the cherry?" he shouted.

A thirty-eight-person cacophony of "No's" answered him.

"Sergeant Peterson, go tell the L.T. the platoon is going

on a SAR (search and recovery) mission for the cherry and we'll be right back."

Moans came up from the troops as they got to their feet.

"At ease that shit," Perry said. "Come on, let's go dig his ass out of the snow."

The platoon moved out across the drop zone into a police call line, without having to be told to do so. They knew what to do. At a double arms-length, the line started moving from the middle of the drop zone toward the beginning. They all knew they put you in the door on your cherry blast. You go out first—there is no other choice. So, if he lawn-darted, and hadn't been able to recover his equipment, he was somewhere close to the beginning of the zone. We all trudged through the snow. Occasionally, someone would have to stop and adjust their snowshoe bindings, but for the most part we made good progress. Our line approached the piles of dead wood created from clearing the area and I heard someone say for the platoon to turn around and start back the other way.

"At ease that!" Sergeant Perry yelled. "Ground your snowshoes and when everybody's ready, we'll work our way over this dead fall."

Murmurings of "freakin' cherry," "this is bullshit," and "I'm going to kick his ass when we find him," scattered throughout the line.

The men stacked their snowshoes neatly in teepees of four and got back on line.

"Let's go!" Perry shouted. "Slowly, a lot of this stuff is rotten."

I grasped the first limb I could and started pulling myself up. The deadfall was about 8 to 10 feet tall, 100 yards wide, and 20 yards deep. Of the thirty-eight searchers, we spread out and had the whole width easily covered. It was just a matter of getting all of us across it.

Once I got on top, it wasn't as easy as I thought. The rubber, vapor barrier (VB) boots we wore didn't provide much traction on frozen tree trunks and limbs. I really felt we were wasting our time. That is, until Daniel Abercrombie started shouting for Sergeant Perry. I figured he had got himself stuck between a couple of the tree limbs, or maybe cut himself on a jagged branch.

That wasn't the case.

I could see Perry's figure working its way toward Daniel. Everyone else in the line seemed to be gravitating toward him too.

"Stand fast, hold your positions," Perry commanded.

Daniel was the soft-spoken son of an Iowa beet farmer. If you met him, you would never expect that the strawberry blond, freckle-faced kid was a specialist in firearms and knew more ways to kill you with a knife than you knew how to die. Even though I was only about twenty yards from him, I couldn't hear what he was saying to Sergeant Perry. The two gathered in that spot for a few seconds, then Daniel turned and started walking back in the direction we came.

"Listen up!" Perry yelled. "Slowly, start making your way over to me. Slowly!"

Everyone in the line turned and started moving his way. One at a time, they approached him. He quietly said something, and then they turned and followed the trail Daniel had forged, back out of the dead fall and toward the trucks. It was still very dark, but the ground contrasts revealed a small gap in the pile where Perry stood. The third man in front of me stopped, then the second, then the first. I still couldn't make out the whispers from Perry. As I stepped up, I made eye contact with him. It was dark. It was desolate. It was cold. His eyes were cold. He leaned forward, close to my face and whispered, "Never forget this."

I looked into the hole.

His name had been Stephen Gray. Stephen Anthony Gray, the priest later read at the invocation. He lay in a perfect parachute exit position, in the impact hole, atop hard, jagged, crushed branches. His elbows tucked to his sides, feet and knees together, right hand gripping his reserve parachute ripcord handle. The white steel helmet, painted with tiny, red cherries, had almost pinched the top of his head off from its final impact with a large log. It looked like it had been put into a vice and flattened to about six inches wide. There was a large, dark spot in the snow surrounding his head. It was a colorless shadow in reality, but it's always crimson in my dreams. He stared at me bug-eyed, the water on his corneas completely frozen. I turned and made my way back silently to where I had left my rucksack.

When I arrived, I noticed everyone was gathering their gear and loading it onto the trucks. I did the same without being told to. Within twenty minutes, we were all loaded, warm inside the back of the truck. Heater blowing. No wind. No ice.

I felt guilty for being happy to get a ride back to the barracks. This convenience had been an expensive one, and not worth it. The trucks bumped and wobbled their way through the forest and back onto the paved road leading to the main fort. We passed through the main gates, down past headquarters, past the artillery garrison, past the M.P.'s barracks, and past our own barracks. We turned by the power station and headed down the main road toward Elmendorf Air Force Base. As we drove, the silence persisted, the warmth engulfed us, and some of us slept.

The trucks pulled around to the parachute staging area known as Green Ramp and stopped. Silently we filed off the trucks and gathered in the hanger to wait for the debriefing and confirmation that the field exercise was cancelled. Most of us sat down on the benches and waited for whatever was going to happen, to happen. It was quiet and cold. Somewhere in the other part of the warehouse I heard a gas engine start up and the whine of hydraulics under a heavy load. My eyes closed and I listened.

It was getting closer.

I opened my eyes and saw a forklift dropping a loaded pallet near the door. The vehicle spun around and disappeared from view, the engine sounds becoming faint and then nothing.

The pallet sat, its load wrapped in clear plastic. One of the other jumpmasters approached it and with his K-bar knife cut away the thin skin revealing the insides.

A new pallet stacked with parachutes near the door.

I heard the growl of a C-130's propellers somewhere off in the distance.

I closed my eyes again.

After talking for some time with the lieutenant, Sergeant Perry came back in. "Gentlemen—let's get geared up, combat equipment, same placement, same sticks. They want to put our knees back in the breeze. Any questions?"

He stood for a moment, waiting to see doubt; disagreement; discontent.

Silence prevailed. After all, I knew what it meant when I buried my low-quarters—we are all dead men.

Sergeant Peterson added, "Okay, gear up. Let's get it right this time."

And we did.

For the sake of the dead.

And I assure you, Malamute drop zone is haunted.

THE GRAVE DWELLERS

MANILA'S CEMENTERIO DEL NORTE
Philippines, circa 1991

THE WATER WAS GLASS. Its stillness was most striking to me. Silent and alone, I stood looking down from
the lip of aircraft elevator number one into this jade-colored
mirror. It reflected the panorama of my image and that of
the ship I served, the US aircraft carrier *Nimitz*. The Sia-
mese twin that lay below me was a pristine version of
Nimitz joined at the waterline and my tiny face looking
up from the surface. Our bow wake rippled closely, in what
seemed to be the ship's deliberate attempt to not disrupt
this deception. Suddenly, a school of flying fish shattered
the image and scattered across like echoes, their shards
skipping and then disappearing in unison.

Solid glass again.

I had traveled across the Pacific Ocean, past Hawaii
and Saipan, Okinawa and Taiwan, and through the South

China Sea. Soon, I would be stopping in Singapore and Thailand, but the most intriguing would be Hong Kong. This is where my distant relative, Henry Pottinger, was the first British governor to rule over the province. There I planned on climbing Pottinger's Peak and overlook Hong Kong to Big Wave Bay. At this point I had become acquainted with the Pacific wind and water. I understood our relationship. Something only awakened sailors truly comprehend.

The ship had started our harbor approach to Subic Bay, Philippines around 03:00 and I was relieved of my duties at 05:00. It was in total darkness that I took my place on the side elevator and waited for the island's unveiling. Except for me, the entire hanger deck was devoid of life; the other sailors were either at their watch station, in the galley for breakfast, or sleeping.

As night finally gave way, the navigator set a narrow course between Grande Island's Fort Wint and the western shore of the bay. While modern construction had begun on Grande Island in the early 1900s, during World War II, Fort Wint was the most important defensive structure for Subic Bay. It was fortified with artillery to protect the dry docks at Olongapo and to guard the Allied Forces at Bataan from a Japanese naval attack from the rear. The waters we sailed, and the soil we passed, and the air we breathed had witnessed the deaths of thousands here. The Philippines has been attacked from all sides and from every country that has ever tried to claim this incredible island. From the Philippine Revolution, Spanish American War, World War I and World War II, the Philippine Islands have seen untold amounts of violence and death.

Fueled by the tales of Tarzan and Robinson Crusoe, I had imagined the jungles of the South Pacific to be lush with vegetation, towering tree canopies, and teaming with wildlife. The sunrise on this morning changed that fantasy. We silently steamed inbound and from my vantage point Subic Bay's western shore lay before me. I was shocked—the sun's rays revealed only a wasteland consisting of the remnants of a dismembered and strewn hardwood forest, apparently clear-cut decades ago. The hills were nothing more than eroded gouges of scraggly, brown undergrowth and closely severed rosewood and mahogany tree stumps. What looked to be miles away were green highlands, but here, the stumps were scattered like neglected tombstones entangled with weed and vines. I looked back across the hanger bay and through the open doors of elevator three. Gliding along the other side I saw Grande Island. From my position, it didn't look much better.

It was then that I realized my goal to visit Manila's Cementerio del Norte was strangely appropriate. This graveyard is also known as the cemetery of the living...

It is certainly rare for any American to visit the Philippines. Except for the various branches of the military and the persons that support them, Americans do not place Subic Bay high on their bucket list. But as a sailor, it was certainly on mine. For a sailor, the Philippines hold a sense of mystery, adventure, and strategic value. Throughout its entire history, the world's militaries have fought over the islands and hundreds of thousands of soldiers and sailors have died there, soaking the land with their blood and discarding their remains across the country. It is not uncommon for farmers or land developers to unearth remains of fighting men or their weapons; warfare is part of the Filipino culture.

When we moored pier side, I was down the gangway at the first bell.

What you might not know is that the Philippine Islands are filled with mysteries, legend and lore, most of which originate from the many religious beliefs brought here by conquering peoples, from verbal histories and urban legends, and also from the accounts of many wars. Every continent has had its wars, but the Philippines are unique. The modern warfare brought to these islands during World War II was quicker, more massive and brutal compared to anything the Filipino people had ever known before.

While you can trace war atrocities committed by individuals in various countries' militaries, it is rare in modern times for abuses committed against the civilian population to be sanctioned or even encouraged by officials. However, this is exactly what happened during the expansion of the Japanese Empire during their massive and violent assaults in the Pacific Rim. Their desire to control everything from the Alaskan Aleutian Islands through the mid-Pacific, to the Philippines and countries of the Far East, to include the massive country of China, fueled their abuses. In doing so, the Japanese Empire outpaced their supply lines. Soon, all branches of the Japanese military were short of weapons, fuel, and food. Food being a particular personal challenge for the individual soldier. Cases of widespread cannibalism were rumored throughout the Far East, especially in China where the Chinese people were terrified of Japanese soldiers.

Even though the US military was aware of cannibalism, it did not address the issue after the Japanese surrender simply because they did not believe the American people would ever forgive the Japanese. Therefore, the US government would not be able to capitalize on the Japanese Empire's war spoils and be paid to rebuild the country. Some of these cannibalistic events are chronicled by the actual Japanese soldiers that committed the offenses in James Brady's novel *Flyboys: A True Story of Courage*.

But still, the Philippines are not a stranger to cannibalism. The indigenous peoples of the Philippines were not widespread cannibals like those of Polynesia or New Guinea; however, it did happen and was mainly ritualistic. What the Filipinos did prize was the act of headhunting. It was a display of manhood, dominance of the body and soul of the enemy, and a symbol or trophy of the warrior's greatness. This was practiced well into the 1930s among the Ilongot people of the mountainous Luzon region and ultimately had to be outlawed and suppressed by the US Army.

Once I was off the ship, I walked down the wharf about a quarter mile to a street leading off Naval Base (NAVSTA) Subic Bay. After clearing the checkpoint, I found myself on the famous bridge over Shit River. Shit River is actually just a tributary name for the Santa Rita River and drainage channel for river overflow and sewage from Olongapo. Right there, as promised by so many other sailors I have spoken to, were the young boys swimming in the filth and the sailors who threw coins into the water for the kids to dive down and retrieve. Laughing and making fun, these sailors were some of the worst ambassadors of the US occupation.

I moved on.

Once on the Olongapo side, there were people everywhere and the smell of the condensed humanity and sewage from the river was almost overwhelming. The crowds of people were trying to sell everything from t-shirts to transvestites. I snaked my way through textile merchants and prostitutes, pimps and Catholic nuns, and of course the food vendors. As soon as I could, I grabbed the first Tuk Tuk I saw. These, I believed at the time, were a great way to negotiate the city. I figured that with their small size, basically a three-wheeled motorcycle, they would be the best way to get through the horrific traffic in Olongapo. I told the driver of a red Tuk Tuk covered with glued-on plastic trinkets and toys that I wanted to get a bus to Manila. He nodded and I got aboard. The driver took me on a fascinating and somewhat scary ride through the streets of Olongapo. Speeding between cars and through red lights, he took me down straight avenues and winding dirt streets. Within moments I was completely disoriented. Finally, we came to a stop in a throng of other Tuk Tuk drivers in a dirty back alleyway. I got out and pulled out my wallet as the other drivers surrounded us. My Tuk Tuk driver was staring at me flatly. I opened my wallet and pulled out a ten-dollar bill. The crowd drew a little closer. As I held it out toward him, he shook his head and pointed at my wallet. I opened the mouth of it, so he could see the remaining fifty dollars. He reached in and took it all. I closed my wallet and turned, heading back out of the alley; the crowd parted, and I heard them laughing as I quickly vacated.

Ten minutes in Olongapo and I was already robbed and lost...

I was lucky that I had listened to one of my more experienced shipmates. He had told me to carry only a few ten-dollar bills in my wallet, and my real money elsewhere. The idea is to have enough in your wallet to satisfy the robber, so they don't feel the need to search the rest of your body.

Regrouping my senses, I retrieved my handy sailor tourist map of Olongapo and got to work. It took about another hour for me to find a bus terminal of sorts that provided transportation to and from Manila. I purchased my ticket and was shortly on my way in a thirty-year-old bus with standing room only. I do not recommend standing for the three-hour drive to Manila. I had to stoop half of the time to look out at the countryside, of which some sections matched my imagination of South Pacific jungles. But with all the swerves and bumps, by the time we arrived in Manila, I was exhausted and a little carsick.

Once off the bus, I grabbed the first "real" taxi I saw and after a ten-minute ride I found myself standing across the street from one of the nastiest and cruelest places I have ever seen: Cementerio del Norte. The cemetery was once located outside the city but with catastrophic overpopulation caused by the religious prohibition of birth control, it is now encompassed by it. It looked to me to be over 100 acres and appeared to house thousands of Manila's poorest people. For the last one hundred years, people are born here, live out their lives, and die in this disgusting place, never knowing anything else. While there are hundreds of cemeteries in the predominately Catholic country, all of which display white painted mini-mausoleums with colorful plaster statues of Jesus or The Virgin Mary, Cementerio del Norte has developed a culture of property squatting and a subclass of grave dwellers.

It was just before noon when I walked through the gates and onto the cemetery grounds. I covered a very small area of the cemetery on my visit, but I hoped it was the worst part. I could hardly see the ground in some areas, the trash was so thick. Most of the mausoleums were stacked four high and made of non-reinforced concrete walls, with the grave dwellers building their stick and cardboard homes on top. Some standalone graves were painted colorfully but most were not. And most showed some signs of criminal mischief damage if not outright grave robbing. Discarded and decaying caskets were stacked from place to place. It appeared that survivors of the deceased actually came into the cemetery to look for old graves, disinter the remains, leave them in the walkways, and bury their own loved ones in their place, cementing

In the Philippines, thousands of people live in cemeteries with the dead. Bodies are routinely disinterred and thrown aside to make dwellings for the living.

the graves closed once again. Standing pools of black water, garbage, and human excrement were in many of the corners where the mausoleums came together. These appeared to be the favorite areas for the children to play soccer with makeshift balls. In some sections, on the top of the fourth level of containers, were huge concrete skull and crossbones where I saw more than one set of lovers holding hands or leaning on one another, looking as if they were waiting for something.

I was not more than twenty paces in before I saw my first discarded human bone—probably a femur. In the next two hours, I saw hundreds, including several skulls. As I made my way through the wall maze of stacked graves, the stench was unbearable. But oddly enough, the wretched people in this place went about their day normally as if in a modern western city.

It was probably thirty minutes before I was confronted by my first hostile vagrant. Within the first hour, my first prostitute offering. And soon after that, the kids started following me begging for anything. I realized I was causing unwanted attention and thought I should get out of there. I asked one of the kids where a McDonald's was, and fifteen minutes later I was out of there and the kid was five dollars richer.

Once I washed my hands then sat down with my food, I regretted this trip to Cementerio del Norte. I had thought if I took the trip, I might be able to better understand death and its myths. I thought maybe the Filipino people I would meet would somehow clarify this through their traditions and lore. I thought I would hear tales of the ghosts in Cementerio del Norte, or how legend described them. I thought I would find out more about the Multo. I knew only that Multo came from the Spanish word "muerto," meaning dead, and I knew that this spirit returned to the land of the living for revenge, to complete a final task, or because of an improper burial. I thought maybe I would meet someone who could tell me about the vampire Manananggal who preys on pregnant women, or the shapeshifting Aswang who loves to eat unborn fetuses and the hearts and livers of small children. I thought maybe I would hear stories about how the Aswang befriended a family member or actually killed a friend and became their doppelganger, tricking the victim's family.

I got none of that.

What I saw were people merely surviving day-by-day, living amongst and sometimes in the same space as the dead. Human remains strewn about and disregarded as nothing of consequence. What I heard were the sounds of despair surrounded by the rumble of vehicle engines and the other echoes of Manila surrounding this place. And what I felt was danger—not from the legends, but from my fellow humans.

As if it were all normal.

I can affirmatively say I found no ghosts in Manila. Except for the ones I brought back with me.

I threw away my shoes.

DIARIES OF A PARANORMALIST

THE ARMED FREIGHTER, SS *THISTLEGORM*

OFF THE COAST OF RAS MUHAMMAD, Egypt in the Red Sea, circa 1985

THE SAILORS WERE SCATTERED ABOUT THE DECKS, half dressed, trying to get any kind of relief from the sweltering heat. Even though it was the first week of October in 1941, they were, after all, moored in the Red Sea, just off the coast of Egypt. Even though it was one o'clock in the morning, the metal ship they sailed upon had collected a good twelve hours of heat from the previous day's sun. This heat was still trying to escape the ship's confines through every open porthole, hatch, and doorway. The sailors' escape was to find any cool piece of steel to lie upon and try to get some uninterrupted sleep. If even for an hour.

Egypt is one of those desert countries with vast temperature variations going from day to night. I have witnessed one hundred and fifteen degrees in the day and forty-five at night, the change occurring in just under three hours. Although October in Egypt may average eighty-five degrees, sitting in the ship on the Red Sea in eighty-degree water, in this steel box, the interior spaces heat up like an oven. And in 1941, there were no air conditioners on board—sailors had to make do.

This particular ship, the British SS *Thistlegorm*, commanded by Captain William Ellis, had been moored here at Safe Anchorage F since September. She was a 400-foot cargo vessel named after the Blue Thistle of Scotland; in Gaelic it is called *Thistlegorm*. She was a simple design, with a simple crew, waiting on orders to proceed to the British controlled Port of Alexandria, Egypt. The ship had originally left Glasgow, Scotland in June and to avoid German and Italian naval and air forces in the Mediterranean, had joined a convoy sailing around the Horn of Africa, through the Indian Ocean and into the Red Sea. A ship collision in the Suez Canal was the holdup and at this moment, no ships could get through to the Mediterranean. So here they sat, anchored with their escort, the light cruiser HMS *Carlisle*, waiting for the word to proceed.

The SS *Thistlegorm*, while being an average supply ship, did not hold within her hull an average cargo. It was a cargo of meaning, one that would certainly influence the effectiveness of the allied forces. There were numerous trucks, motorcycles, armored vehicles, machine guns, rifles, ammunition, railway wagons and locomotives, aircraft parts, and uniform items, all destined for the Western Desert Force, the newly named Eighth Army. These supplies were part of a package that was to help curtail German advances in the region.

The night of October 6th was clear. Blankets of stars brightened the sky and their reflections glimmered on the wakeless Red Sea. None of the sailors who took notice of the distant plane engines felt any fear. The sound would have been common in their area and would not have been much of a warning of danger. However, in recent days the German Intelligence Corps realized there was a large buildup of Allied troops in the area and dispatched two Heinkel bomber planes to search out and destroy the troop carrier they believed was transiting along the African coast. Flying out of Crete, the two German aircraft searched until their fuel forced them to abandon the mission. To cover more area on their return, they split and headed back on two different courses. One of these aircraft's engine was what the *Thistlegorm* sailors heard.

As the sound got closer, some of the crew might have sat up on an elbow to scan the sky. Some might even have stood or began running when they heard the distinct sound of a plane making a dive-bombing run, its engines becoming louder and higher pitched. One or two of the Royal Navy gun crewmembers may even have reached the anti-aircraft battery, but it was too late. The German pilot put two bombs straight into the number four hold of the *Thistlegorm*—the explosion practically cut the entire stern off, nearly splitting the vessel in two. The explosion cut much of the superstructure away and tossed the two locomotive engines to either side of the vessel. Within minutes, the ship, its contents, and some of its crew lay beneath one hundred feet of ocean water.

Out of the forty-two crewmen, four sailors and five Royal Navy gunners were killed.

You see, it wasn't until forty-four years later that I discovered the *Thistlegorm* had ever existed. I had never heard of her until my first weekend of liberty and my casual discussion with a local fisherman about good places to scuba dive. I had no idea of the importance of this ship, her mission, or her loss.

So, there I hovered, twenty or so feet above the ship's bow, windlass, and anchor chains, waiting for my scuba diving partner to clear his ears and descend to me. He was a French paratrooper assigned to the United Nations Multinational Force and Observers in the Sinai Desert and the only other scuba diver I could find at the South Camp near Sharm El Sheik. I knew I was there for only a few weeks to help relieve the regulars stationed there, but when I spoke with some other locals and they too told me of the *Thistlegorm*, I knew, no matter what, I had to go.

In the Red Sea, the skeleton of the *SS Thistlegorm* and its crew await diver's explorations.

The water around the wreck was a bluish green with fifty or so feet of visibility. During both of my two dives, a current ran strong from bow to stern. It was the first large wreck I had ever explored and the experience for this twenty-year-old was overwhelming. I had dived many hours in Alaska and many times in completely black water; however, the currents here, the huge structure, the torn metal, and strange fish were absolutely surreal.

My dive partner, we will call him Pierre (I don't remember his name), and I both rented some antiquated scuba equipment from a commercial dive shop and had no problems hiring one of the many fishing boats to take us out. The dive equipment looked twenty years old and as if it had never been serviced. The dual hose regulators along with dual steel scuba tanks were of some concern but we set out anyway—at that time, I wasn't that smart.

Once Pierre joined me, we made a slow fly over the deck from bow to stern, letting the current do the work. I saw more wildlife on this one dive than I had seen in almost one hundred dives in Alaska. There were large schools of small silver, yellow, and pink fish darting across the structure, turtles flying by, lion fish hovering above corals attached to the deck and railings, spotted, striped, solid-colored fish of all shapes and sizes, but what struck me most was the cargo. This ship still had its cargo. Within each hold we could see the rusted trucks and motorcycles, crates of ammunition, artillery shells, scattered boots, an aircraft radial engine, and rifles red with rust that were fused together as one clump. Something struck me about these vehicles. They were completely rusted, red all over, yet their tires were still black and looked as if they were the only things in this catastrophe to survive.

Resisting the urge to stop, we continued on, descending until the ship's deck fell away from us, where the bomb actually exploded and almost cut the ship in two. Ripped metal and scattered wreckage reached up from the gaping hole. We descended farther, gliding over more of the supplies and debris until we came to the stern and located the deck and anti-aircraft guns there, somewhere in about one hundred feet of water. We paused. Though the lights we had rented were poor, the sun's rays still reached this depth and provided sinister shadows of movement all over the wreck. We had no underwater camera. Cell phones had not yet been invented. It was just us and the wreck.

As I hovered there, breathing the stale air from these old steel scuba tanks, I imagined the explosion. The fire. The ship folding in half and swallowing water. I imagined the chaos and the screams. The men she took with her to the bottom. Men possibly trapped somewhere inside. Long decayed by now. I could imagine seeing them on the deck. Right in front of me.

We started back up the starboard side, up past what looked like cabins and maybe the wheelhouse. Off farther to my right, I could see one of the locomotive engines sitting on the sea bottom with other materials strewn about. Soon we were at the bow again, and then on the surface— our fisherman drifting close by.

As I handed my equipment up into the boat, I could not help but be distracted by the sea surrounding us. I looked all around and imagined that night. Imagined the men who survived the bombing, struggling in the water, swimming toward the safety of HMS *Carlisle*. Captain Ellis and another of his crew were later awarded for their heroic acts that morning. Yet, nine men had been killed. Dead, right at this spot.

While in the coming weeks I was fortunate enough to dive many different places along the Red Sea, I never again experienced the awe and wonder of my first sight of the bow of the *Thistlegorm*. Several weeks later, I dove the wreck again with two American soldiers, but the current had stirred up silt around the wreck and the visibility was only about twenty feet. With my dive partners being inexperienced sport divers, we spent most of our time around the bow and near the first cargo hold. I never got the opportunity to enter the wreck and explore. This would be my second and final dive on the ship.

When I was there, the ship was only known to a few of the locals. Today, it is the most popular wreck dive in the Middle East. Dozens of ships anchor their boats to the

Thistlegorm's chains, pulling on the already fragile vessel, every day. Thousands of scuba divers from all over the world go there to dive, explore, and take home trinkets from the ship. As I searched the internet for the fate of the historic site, I found dozens of scuba diving articles, blog postings, a few books, and a virtual tour of the ship. I saw many photos of divers swarming over her rusted railings, superstructure, and cargo holds. Divers so numerous they had to form underwater queues in order to get a chance at seeing a part or entering the ship, even just for a few minutes.

I have dived several wrecks worldwide, and as you can imagine, it is difficult if not impossible to spend enough time submerged to do any real paranormal research. On my first *Thistlegorm* dive, it was awe-inspiring. Mesmerizing. It was a surreal experience diving over the ship, bow to stern—the sea life accompanying her was vast. But as I see her now, her internet presence and YouTube videos, I can't help but think that the *Thistlegorm* and her crew are at peace. And it seems to me, in the case of the *Thistlegorm*, the living is the one haunting the dead.

DIARIES OF A PARANORMALIST

AWA'UQ

MASSACRE AT REFUGE ROCK
Three Saints Bay (Бухта Трёх Святителей), Alaska, circa 1984

IN THE SPRING OF 1984, shortly after "break up," when the ice loosened its hold on the land, I was fortunate enough to attend an abbreviated pararescue course at Coast Guard Air Station, Kodiak, Alaska. The training, a project of the Alaskan Department of the Interior, was an amalgamation of US Army land navigation and river fording instruction, US Air Force pararescue medical treatment and transport training, and US Coast Guard helicopter rescue-swimmer delivery and recovery techniques. Throughout that spring and summer, I traveled and saw enough of the Alaskan wilderness along with the Gulf of Alaska to last a lifetime; however, as I get older, I often find myself longing to return.

After concluding the first week of training, I avoided the standard 19-year-old soldier's tradition of spending the entire weekend in some form of intoxication and found myself standing in front of the Kodiak Historical Society's Baranov Museum. I had walked upon the building simply by chance as I was trying to make my way down to the inner harbor to view the fishing fleet. The structure was renovated from the original Russian-American magazin (storage facility) built by the Russian-American Company in the early 1800s. After several hours in the museum, I discovered that while Kodiak was established in 1793, the Russians had occupied the original settlement of Three Saints Bay in 1784, approximately 60 miles south. This occupation occurred after fur trader Grigory Shelikhov and 130 Russian cannoneers of the Shelikhov-Golikov Company reportedly fired upon and massacred over 500 indigenous men, women, and children of the Alutiiq people at Refuge Rock. I was told it was considered a sacred and taboo site named by the Alutiiq people as Awa'uq. The Alutiiq language meaning: "Where one becomes numb."

I had to go there.

In the ensuing few weeks, I attended my training and did my best to read up on the massacre. Like so many other atrocities, the winning faction typically gets to write the history, and the massacre at Refuge Rock is a perfect example. You see, the Russians had been having continued trouble with the Aleut and Alutiiq peoples for years. Simply put, the Russians wanted fur and the

Aleuts and Alutiiq wanted them to stay away. While it was reported by the Russians that the Aleuts and Alutiiq had previously attacked Russian ships to drive them away from the area, they would be of little threat to a Russian force with guns. One of the worst examples of the most violent contacts happened in 1761 when the Russian ship *Sv. Gravil* attacked a band of Aleuts. Two years later, in response to the killings, the Aleuts counterattacked the Russians and sank four of their boats and killed over 150 Russians.

Grigory Shelikhov was aware of this attack, even though it was over 20 years prior. He relied on the blessing of the Russian government, and exaggerated the continuing threat of these people's spears and arrows against his ships' cannons and muskets. In April of 1784, he and his men assaulted the Alutiiq's position at Refuge Rock, a place the indigenous peoples would flee when they felt threatened. That of course is a clue to what they felt was the Russians' intent, and the fact that they brought all their women and children, which they would not have done had they intended to go to war.

Strange as it may seem in the continental United States, transport by airplane in Alaska is not only preferred, it is most times easier than overland and very commonplace. It was so in this case, for sure. There are only two ways into Old Harbor, by plane or boat.

After withdrawing my entire paycheck, all three hundred and twenty dollars of it, I took one week of leave after my training. I went to a small nearby airport and paid a bush pilot who made routine round trips to Old Harbor. He charged forty dollars for a round trip flight there—this was an early Alaskan Uber. He flew a red, taildragger Cessna with huge over-inflated tires. It was old and looked like it had been caught in a hailstorm more than once. Just before we took off, I saw him wiping spattered engine oil off the outside of his windshield. Having never been in such a plane before, I figured oil on the windshield was normal...

I think the scraggly bearded old bastard said ten words to me during the trip both there and back, but the ultimate view was every bit worth the money. The gray cloud ceiling was about 1500 feet, so he flew relatively low, east of the Kodiak mountains and west of the coast all the way to the long dirt road that served as Old Harbor's airport. The plane fought its way against strong sea winds and soared over green inlets and bays, snowcapped ridges and forests, and rocky shores scattered with thousands of seabirds. This was my first good look at Alaska from the air. I did not want it to end, but it did. He taxied to the end of the runway and turned the plane around, unlatching the door; the air thrust from the propeller flipped the door up under the wing and held it there. He said, "Two o'clock every day," and pointed out the door. I grabbed my Army issued rucksack and followed his direction, stepping into the gray mud of the road. I chose a direction and then headed onto what looked to be the only road into town. Looking back, I saw him hanging out on the strut, wiping more engine oil away. After several minutes walking, I heard his plane engine speed up and he was off down the runway.

I checked my watch; it was two o'clock.

As I got my bearings, I realized the town was even smaller than I had imagined. The long and skinny structures making up the community were nestled snugly between the mountains and the sea, maybe three feet above sea level. The striking blue domes of the Russian Orthodox Church stood out above all else. They were simply odd and completely out of place.

Soon, I found a small "Bates" motel of sorts for thirty dollars a night and checked in. The proprietors there were as talkative as my pilot, but they did point me to the docks where there was no shortage of small boat operators willing to take individuals fishing, sightseeing, or in my case, across the bay to a long-forgotten place.

This story would be better if I could remember his name, but I chose an old Alaskan, probably of Russian descent, who when I mentioned the massacre to a group of boat operators, immediately said he knew the place. His enthusiasm was encouraging; however, we had some negotiating to do. He charged by the hour and I just needed a ride across the bay. My plan was to have a boat take me across to Sitkalidak Island, and I would walk approximately five miles to the rock. He would have none of that and told me he would take me all the way to the rock tomorrow for one hundred dollars. One hundred dollars was simply out of my reach; I still had to pay for food and lodging, get myself back to Kodiak, and then on to Anchorage within five days.

I changed the subject to the original colony of Three Saints Bay. He pointed south, away from Sitkalidak and said he would take me there for sixty dollars. I had planned on only spending a hundred dollars and was honest and told him.

He asked how long I was staying. I told him two days. He suggested that tomorrow, if I wanted to see the rock, he could take me to the strand through McDonald Bay for sixty and the following day to Three Saints Bay for a total of one hundred twenty dollars. I remembered that McDonald Bay was the same route as the attacking Russians used to ambush their victims. Immediately I agreed; I figured I would just spend one night less in a hotel room and work out the logistics later.

We agreed, and he told me to meet him at 7:00 am, even though the sun did not set until around 10:00 pm. I too decided it would be best to get an early start. Plus, it was his boat and he seemed to be the only boat captain enthusiastic about going.

The money I spent of my three hundred and twenty bought me one of the best memories of my life.

It was also one of my biggest disappointments.

That night, I did not sleep well. I kept thinking about some of the things I had read while at the museum in Kodiak. How the people, warriors, old men, women and children, had fled to the rock for safety. How the reports were between 300 and 3,000 native Alaskans dead and not a single injured of the 130 Russian men. How women had jumped into the sea—how they had thrown their children into the sea, so they would not become Russian slaves. I thought about the man that had survived the attack and later told a Finnish naturalist about it:

"The Russians went to the settlement and carried out a terrible bloodbath. Only a few were able to flee to Angyahtalek in baidarkas; 300 Koniags were shot by the Russians. This happened in April. When our people revisited the place in the summer the stench of the corpses lying on the shore polluted the air so badly that none could stay there, and since then the island has been uninhabited. After this, every chief had to surrender his children as hostages; I was saved only by my father's begging and many sea otter pelts." - Arsenti Aminak

Over three hundred Alutiiq men, women, and children were massacred by Russian fur traders at Refuge Rock – The place where one goes numb.

Whether it is 1784 or 2018, technology and power in all its forms do not change the fact that humans are still, biologically speaking, nothing more than animals.

At 6:50 am, I arrived at the docks and saw there were several other people already on the boat preparing for a fishing excursion. The captain welcomed me onboard at 7:00 am. I stepped over the gunnel with my backpack containing only a towel, an extra coat, a canteen of water, and some cheese and summer sausage—just enough for a short outing.

His boat was apparently some sort of wooden commercial fishing vessel twenty years prior. Maybe thirty-five feet long with a small forward cabin and large aft deck area for nets, it was certainly sturdy. While it had a new coat of white paint with blue trim, there was not a single wood plank that did not show scars of foul weather, deck scrapes, or mooring impacts. Once underway, we crossed the bay. He pointed as we passed Fang Point and cruised about five miles, then turned south into McDonald Bay. The fishermen busied themselves preparing their equipment, but for the most part were quiet. I am guessing from hangovers.

The morning was overcast and the sea state about three free, but much calmer once we entered the lagoon. There were multiple varieties of birds crossing the sky, but on the water surface only the dark blue covering moved.

At this point, I realized the captain was much wiser than I initially gave him credit; it would have taken me a full day of hiking to make it across the Sitkalidak Island hills to the land spit that blocked the lagoon from Partition Cove, Refuge Rock and the Northern Pacific Ocean.

He navigated his boat over to a small outcropping about a thousand feet from the end of the lagoon and let me off at the bow. As I went over the side, he paused, then he asked me if I had a gun. I told him that I did not. The fishing group broke out into laughter. He looked away, shaking his head and throttled up, heading back to Old Harbor with the intent of meeting me back here in eight hours.

After several minutes' walk south, I arrived at the strand that connects the main Sitkalidak Island to what I call the East Sitkalidak Island. The strand is only maybe a thousand feet long and a couple hundred feet wide. It might be three feet above high tide. If this strand were not here, the landmasses would certainly be two separate islands.

I wondered why my captain had asked if I was armed. Sitkalidak is a relatively small and isolated island in the Kodiak group. I could not imagine there would be any bear here. After all, there is no game for a bear to hunt. And of course, I was 19 years old. And an idiot.

I looked back as my ride disappeared around the first bend.

I was alone at Awa'uq: the place where one becomes numb.

As I surveyed my surroundings, the sea breeze pulled at my coat and caused the stiff grasses that covered this place to whistle. The land here is sparse with only grass, small bushes, and a scraggly tree here and there. The hills of the island rise here on both sides, carved with deep ravines from millennia of melting snows, and their tops, though not very high, were from time to time shrouded in mist. On both sides, muddy, gray fluid bled from the remains of this melting ice and flowed through the gorges and into the patiently waiting bay and ocean.

I decided to get a good look at Refuge Rock, so I walked down to the beach. It is hard to describe the image of the rock from there. Because of the mists, it was not clear. Because of the churning seas, it was not placid. I can only say, it was significantly present, maybe eight hundred to a thousand feet offshore. I could see the island had an ashen and rocky shoreline like Sitkalidak with a rise and surrounding cliff covered in green grasses terminating with a flat, mesa-like top. A good position to throw spears from, but certainly a bad position to receive cannon fire.

Immediately, I got the feeling there had been ancient construction between the strand and the rock. I surveyed my position. It looked like someone had dug soil out of the strand area and deposited it into the water, all the way across to Refuge Rock. It sounds crazy, but I could see this skinny bit of land only a foot or two under the water, just like a submerged road leading there. Behind me on the strand, there was even a depression filled with water, mimicking the remains of a quarry excavation. Had the Alutiiq people constructed a rudimentary causeway to the rock?

I looked back at the ocean waters that blocked my goal. Last night I had resolved that I would not be able to get onto the island since I simply did not have the money for my boat captain to take me there, and of course, my greed for wanting to also go to Three Saints Bay. But now, I knew the island wanted me there. One or two feet below the surface, my road to Refuge Rock stretched before me. It was right there.

The air temperature was in the fifties and the water probably around forty degrees. The seas had at the most, two-foot swells. Based on the condition of the beach, it was possibly approaching low tide. My cold weather indoctrination training told me, if I could keep my torso dry, I could make it. I thought about the mountain climbers of Everest and K2, how they did not allow frostbite or the fact that they could lose their fingers and toes to deter them from achieving their goals. And Refuge Rock was my goal.

I looked down. I was wearing blue jeans. One layer of white socks. A pair of black leather Army boots. A t-shirt covered with a flannel shirt and an insulated windbreaker. Was it possible that this was the plan all along? If I could keep my upper legs and torso dry, I was certain I could make it, assuming the road was level the entire way. I tightened the straps on my backpack.

I took one step into the water. The trail was solid and gravel. And yes, it was damn cold. I took the next step and the next. Forty feet out, with the rise and fall of the waves, the water reached my knees. Fifty feet out, I caught a two-foot swell that pushed me to the side of this narrow path, and the water reached my upper thighs. Three minutes later, I was gathering all the scattered sticks and twigs I could find on the beach and near hillside—once alight, and for the next four hours, I hunkered down out of the wind behind an outcropping of rocks. From there I listened and stared at my island as the fire dried my clothes and warmed my feet.

With a kayak I could have made it there. With a canoe I could have made it there. Hell, with a child's inflatable boat and a single plastic paddle I could have made it there. Of course, by handing over forty more dollars to my captain, I would have made it there for sure.

It was at this point I realized it wasn't going to happen.

I donned my dried clothes and semi-dried boots, and I spent the next three hours scouring the beach for artifacts. I found nothing substantial; time and tides had wiped the area clean of any battle that occurred here in 1784. I am sure that with a metal detector, a person who looked hard enough could at least find scattered shot and ball from the Russians. Or maybe someone with a keen enough eye could locate spear points or arrowheads.

For me, I only discovered two things. One, is the unanswerable question of how it happens that a 19-year-old kid from Texas finds himself alone in this place, and two, understanding the feeling of peaceful regret as the boat arrived to retrieve me.

The next morning, cloud cover was much the same and my captain took me south and then into Three Saints Bay. This time he and I were alone, and I sat with him in the pilothouse. The seas were a constant three feet and there was no way for him to make it close enough to safely put me ashore without grounding his boat. As we passed a section of beach, he pointed at some ancient pilings jetting up from the water, possibly the skeletons of the old pier. He showed me an area that looked like square site locations for the buildings that were once there. He pointed out a place on the hill where there were many rectangular depressions—he believed it was the settlement's original graveyard. There's not much, he said. The earthquake and tsunami destroyed the whole village. They relocated to Kodiak. Whatever was left of buildings, people, and things, the tsunami pulled off the shore and was now directly below us on the ocean bottom.

He only charged me thirty dollars since this time he didn't have to come back to get me.

He dropped me back at the dock and I went to the motel and packed my gear; it was 10:00 am. I checked out and went to a small café near the Russian church where I had a hot cup of coffee and a cinnamon roll. I then headed back to the airport where my red bush plane landed at 1:45 pm.

We were airborne at 2:01 pm.

When the plane lifted into the air, it felt heavier than before. This time I was carrying with me the weight of what could have been. I have always wondered what would have happened had I been brave enough to push myself all the way to the Rock on that submerged road. With mountain climber-like dedication to make the summit. Or like the Alutiiq people themselves that fled there so long ago, enduring the frigid water.

One day, I would like to return to the island. I would like to go to Refuge Rock—Awa'uq, the place where one becomes numb.

I would like to sit there again.

I would like to listen to the grass once more.

Never again will I refuse to pay the total price for a boat ride. The bigger price I ultimately paid was for the experience I missed.

THE ALAMO DEFENDERS

San Antonio, Texas

I FIRST VISITED THE ALAMO in 1975 with my fifth-grade elementary class. Back then, it was treated as a sacred site. While within the walls, visitors observed strict silence and the Alamo staff run by the Daughters of the Republic did not hesitate to remove anyone from the building for talking or causing any kind of distraction. In 2019, that is no longer the case. While the Alamo is still considered by many as a sacred site, talking and laughing among the visitors is commonplace. Now, it is much more like a tourist destination than a pilgrimage. I even heard a high school-aged boy say that in the 1836 battle the defenders of the Alamo got what they deserved from Santa Anna for being traitors against the Mexican government. Which of course from the view of present-day Mexico is true; however, any country's citizens can be expected to rebel against a tyrannical government at any time—it is the nature of things. The comical part of the young man's perspective was that this high schooler left out the fact that several years prior to the massacre at the Alamo, General Antonio López de Santa Anna had rebelled against Spain to obtain Mexico's independence—the very thing the Texans were trying to do for Texas.

Today the Alamo sits in the middle of downtown San Antonio, surrounded by the haunted Emily Morgan, Crockett, and Menger Hotels. It is one of the most famous buildings in the United States. Not only is it a historical and religious site, it is not surprisingly noted as an active paranormal site as well. After all, if you were constructing the formula for a haunting, the Alamo would meet all the criteria; an Indian burial ground, love, betrayal, sacrifice, murder, disillusionment and desecration.

During Mexican rule The Alamo (which means cottonwood tree in Spanish) was referred to as *Misión San Antonio de Valero*, established around 1744. Initially, the mission was used as a garrison for the soldiers that protected the community against raiding Apache and Comanche Indians. At that time, it was actually positioned outside the growing community next to what would one day be the city cemetery. It is believed that there are over a thousand bodies buried under and around the Alamo itself, not only because it was a church but also because at one time it was unofficially the first hospital in Texas. Prior to the War of Independence, there were even plans to tear it and the compound down to prevent the Texans from using it against Mexico.

The battlefield of the Alamo was a huge area around the compound itself. Modern streets, office buildings, and retail shops now cover this place, hiding the history, physical evidence, and the dead as well. Santa Anna laid siege to the Alamo for thirteen days and on March 6, 1836 the Mexican forces entered the compound. Using cannon to breach the barricaded doors of the Alamo's defenders, they entered the garrison and barracks shooting and bayonetting the remaining Texans there. The last to be killed were the defenders manning the cannon in the chapel itself. A contingency of Mexican soldiers fired a coordinated musket volley then charged into the eleven remaining men and finished them off with bayonets. All in all, it is believed that 180 to 250 Texans were killed and 400 to 600 Mexicans, all around this Catholic chapel.

After the battle, Santa Anna ordered the Texans' bodies to be stacked and burned in three separate funeral pyres. The exact location of this cremation was not recorded in any history; however, it is widely believed the incident occurred at the corner of what is now Alamo Plaza and East Houston Street, behind the long barracks, near or under the Alamo Cenotaph monument. It is believed the

Mexican soldiers were removed from the battlefield and buried at the Old Campo Santo near present day Milam Park in San Antonio.

Shortly after the Alamo, the Texans rallied and battled Mexico's armies again, this time defeating their forces and gaining Texas' independence. Within that year, Colonel Juan Seguín travelled to the Alamo and discovered the pyres. He gathered the ash remains and entombed them in San Fernando Cathedral, in present day San Antonio. Many years later, during renovations of the cathedral, the ash remains were discovered and reinterred in a marble tomb and displayed at the cathedral's entrance. This is where they remain today. But that is not the end of the story.

Ghosts of the Alamo's defenders are routinely seen on the grounds of the Alamo and on the streets and in the hotels surrounding it. On the streets, late at night, the sound of horse hooves can be heard and in some cases the sound of chanting is reported. In most of these instances, the original people that reported these ghostly occurrences are not documented, and now the stories fall into the column of legend.

I have spent a lot of time in and around the Alamo. The whole area, the complex, and the Alamo itself has its own feel. Current employees with the Alamo are reluctant to share any of their own experiences to avoid repercussions

Ghostly soldiers still standing their posts and strange shadows are often seen on the grounds of The Alamo.

from either their supervisors or city officials. However, on any given night you can see paranormal enthusiasts using a variety of detection equipment perusing the grounds and the streets surrounding it. I've spent many hours both day and nighttime around the complex. I have yet to employ any of my own paranormal researching techniques on the site itself. I am far more intrigued by the experiences of sensitives and mediums and other visitors.

My only personal experience is that of seeing a reflection of what seemed to be a child peering out of one of the windows. As I walked by, I clearly saw the image. Once I stopped and backed up it was gone. The rational scientific materialist in me explains this experience away by conjuring excuses of why I may have misinterpreted what I saw. I tell myself it could have been a reflection off the glass, a light shimmer, a mirror image of the clouds or the moon. As with many paranormal experiences they are often not duplicated and are fleeting instances. However, while I am not a medium and do not consider myself a sensitive, I do have an oppressive feeling when visiting this place.

The history of the Alamo is long and diverse. It was not only used as a religious Chapel but also as a fort, a place to store grain, and was made into a police headquarters and jail for a time. Even then, the paranormal reports continued. Experiences have caused employees and visitors to hastily depart. And there are many cases where employees quit their jobs and never returned because of the things that they've seen and heard.

It is my belief that if you rid yourself of the disharmony of the city's daily routine and wander the grounds well after midnight, you will learn much more.

THE RED-EYED DEMON

ANAKTUVUK PASS
Alaska, circa 1984

DISCLAIMER: I do not advocate hoaxes. Usually...

PRIVATE BROOKS BROKE THE ICE from the truck's door handle and pulled it open. The night guards should have made sure the doors were thawed and everything in the trucks was warmed at least every half hour. Everyone knew, in twenty below, or any below weather, the night guards were to take the portable, hot air blowing, swing-fire-heaters and warm the moving parts of all the trucks and their tires. On this night, it was sixty below. Without this, the trucks would freeze in place and be useless to the soldiers. That not only meant a tactical mistake, it could also mean death, depending how far you were from civilization, and of course, the severity of the weather.

Brooks pushed the glow-plug button for the truck's diesel engine, and held it in. He could hear the whirring from the heating of the air in the cylinders. After a couple of minutes, he pushed the start button on the floor with his boot. The engine slowly turned over a few revolutions, but it didn't fire. Brooks was only nineteen, but he was a veteran with these Army transports. He could tell right away, the night guards had not done their jobs keeping the equipment warm. He mashed the glow-plug button again and listened to the whirr a few more minutes. This time, as he stomped down on the start button, the engine fired, and his truck belched to life. Black smoke vented from the exhaust, disappearing into the pitch-black night. He allowed the engine to warm itself for about five minutes, until he noticed the temperature gauge starting to rise, and then forced the transmission lever into first gear. The truck growled some but capitulated and he let out the clutch. The big vehicle strained, and then in one jolt forward, collapsed into the snow. Brooks immediately shut down the engine and got out. With his dim, Army issued flashlight, he circled the vehicle and inspected the tires. Each of them had become frozen to the ground during the night, and due to the cold, the rubber was as brittle as glass. When he forced the truck forward, the two front rubber tires shattered into shards and the entire truck sat helpless on its front axles, deep in the Arctic snow. Brooks stepped over the tether line used to guide the soldiers to and from their tents and trucks and headed back toward the maintenance tent. The soldiers rigged tether lines a week prior because of the blinding whiteouts they were experiencing. But tonight was crystal clear, other than the fact you couldn't see your hand in front of your face without a flashlight. It was a true Arctic night.

I had just returned to the platoon's ten-man tent when the field phone made its sickening growl. A three-quarters growl, three-quarters belch, three-quarters squeak, actually. There was only one person awake in the tent, other than me, and that was Sergeant Fegly. He sat, completely encased in his green sleeping bag, zipped to his chin, with the drawstring tight around his skinny face. A paperback book sat in his makeshift lap, between his belly and drawn-up knees. The tent was dimly lit with an Army flashlight pointing at the ceiling, casting a glow not much stronger than a candle. Fegly's eyes didn't leave the page, as the phone rattled a second time. The other nine green cocoons were also motionless, feet toward the center of the round tent, like green petals of a flower. However, this flower, after being in the tundra for three weeks, without a bath, did not have a springtime odor. I closed the tent flap behind me as the third rattle came.

"You want me to get that?" I asked.

The zipper of Fegly's sleeping bag ripped down a few inches, his hand came out, turned the page of his book, then quickly recoiled, and immediately the zipper closed again. I could see Fegly was on the last few pages of the book he started the night before, and apparently didn't want to be bothered.

I had left around ten o'clock on an eight-hour patrol, and now it was a few minutes after six in the morning. Before I left, Fegly had told me a little about the book. Something about an Egyptian Sphinx with red glowing eyes, and demons. I don't know, I really wasn't paying that much attention. By the condition of his surroundings, it was obvious he had been reading all night, and the already twitchy man was as jumpy as ever. A crumpled up half pack of Marlboros sat beside a C-ration can he was using as an ashtray, and his canteen cup was half filled with steaming coffee he warmed over the gasoline-burning Yukon stove. Like normal, along with his naturally squirrelly state, he was nicotined and caffeined up. I stared at him, watching his bugging eyes flick back and forth across the pages as the phone sounded again.

I picked it up and pressed the button. "First platoon, first squad, Specialist Lawson," I said into the receiver.

It was some maintenance supervisor sergeant from the maintenance tent who said, "Tell Sergeant Fegly your duce-and-a-half's tires just shattered, and he needs to come down to the maintenance tent ASAP to help get'em changed."

"Roger that," I said. "Are you going to send someone here to pick him up?"

"Shit, no, the re-supply convoy leaves in one hour and all the vehicles are taken. If you want any warm chow, you tell him to get his ass down here, now."

"I understand," I said. "First platoon out."

The field phones were a curse and a blessing. Without them, if we needed something, we would have to hump our ass through the snow to go and get it; in most cases, we decided we didn't need it that bad. But with them, they could order *you* to hump your ass, instead of coming to get you.

I looked over to Fegly as his arms came out to close the book. "Shit," he whispered.

"I know," I said. "You've got to go down to the maintenance tent. The duce blew all its tires."

"No, man, I mean shit about this book," he whispered again, and stared down at the cover. A golden lion's face with ruby eyes stared back at him.

"Did you hear me? You have to go to the maintenance tent and take care of the truck," I repeated.

"What, the maintenance tent?" he asked.

The idea just popped into my head. I really hadn't thought about doing anything to him on this field exercise. Last time, Sergeant Miller had found the discarded legs from a slaughtered moose and put them into a C-ration box for him to find. When he did, his surprised reaction contained more than just a startled scream; he also threw up. Blew his groceries right there, throwing chunks of the stuff on a couple of guys who had just started eating theirs. And since I don't care much for vomit, I hadn't planned on any further jokes. But now, my mind was working on something else; something that probably wouldn't cause that type of involuntary action; maybe some other reaction, though.

"Yeah, they want you down there to change the tires so it can go with the convoy," I said. "You only have an hour."

"Shit," Fegly repeated, as he clawed his way out of his bag. He scrambled around trying to get his layers of uniforms on.

"I got to take a squirt, I'll talk to ya later," I said, opening the tent flap again.

Fegly was trying to light a cigarette, take a sip of his coffee, and pull his Arctic boots on, all at the same time. I paused for a moment to watch the disaster take place. The boot slipped and fell onto the Yukon stove, the outer rubber melting instantly with the heat. His canteen cup was bumped off his bedroll mat and spilled onto the poor soul that was asleep next to him. Then he almost burnt his eyebrows off with his cigarette lighter. I closed the tent flap as every green petal in our Arctic flower raised in an eruption of threats and curses. I stood up in the crisp, Arctic air and smiled at my ingenuity.

The maintenance tent was about 500 yards through a small, low-lying, wooded area. To simulate battle conditions, the Army scattered the units to avoid massive losses in the case of an aerial attack. Each of these operation areas was connected with the field phones and the tether lines.

Like most early mornings in this latitude, it was still pitch black. I counted on that. I headed at a brisk pace toward the maintenance tent and pulled out a small, cardboard C-ration box I had in my cargo pocket. As best I could, I tore an eight-inch by eight-inch section off the box. I folded it in half and ripped two holes in it, wide enough that I could see through, and then shaped them carefully into the eyes of a demon, like the eyes on Fegly's book cover. Kind of bent teardrops, I guess.

I kept going, looking for the ditch I had seen the day before. It was near a thick group of small bushes, actually trees, but their growth had been stunted by the short growing seasons. I remembered it was about 200 yards from our tent. I pulled out my gas mask and fitted the new eyes into the lenses of the mask. It took a while to get them straight, but I kept trimming the edges as I walked, and finally they fit. The trail dropped off a bit and I found my grove of trees. I couldn't have asked for a better ambush point. I turned my white parka inside out, to expose the dark synthetic faux fur lining, then settled down in the snow to wait for my prey.

I knew it would take Fegly a good ten minutes to get dressed, but once he was on the move, his quick pace would cover the trail in no time. I fished around in my cargo pocket for an illumination stick. It was a small, plastic cylinder filled with chemicals so that when you bent it, they would mix, causing the stick to light up. Each soldier was given several different colored sticks to use in the case of a whiteout, so they would be easier to locate. I found a red one, bent it, and got it going. The red illuminated the snow around me, and I quickly wedged it into the eyeholes of my gas mask. I held it out in front of me and inspected it.

The mask, of which I could only see an outline, stared back at me with angry, red eyes. I sat it in my lap and waited. It took much longer than I expected. I thought he may have found someone to give him a ride, or something to ride on, and he had gone around on the roadway. I was terribly cold, and just as I was about to stand up and head back, I heard something. I held my breath and forced my ears to strain. Some kind of noise, up the trail, toward where I came. It was a rhythmic squeak. The unique squeaking sound of rubber boots on new snow.

I held the mask down, hiding the glow, as to not give

away my position. I strained my eyes through the blackness, searching for a shadowed movement, a wisp of warm, exhaled air, or a shimmer off a canteen cup. But what I saw was a tiny red light. Just a speck, really, bouncing up and down the trail like a fairy light, flying along, coming to me. I tried to focus better, but the cold had thickened the water in my eyes and froze the water around my eyelashes; everything was a bit hazy and created a halo effect. The light was definitely getting closer and it would become brighter at times, and then dim down a little.

The light from his cigarette, I thought, and waited. Sure enough, I could just make out his outline. He was mumbling something to himself as he descended into my lair. Quietly, I pulled on the mask, and then pounced out from behind the trees with a loud and thunderous satanic roar, assisted by my gas mask's vibrating voice emitter. As I landed in the middle of the trail, with my arms outstretched in your standard demonic attack stance, I could see a shower of sparks explode from Fegly's face, as something in his hands inadvertently slapped the cigarette from his mouth. His helmet flew off the back of his head like it was ejected from a fighter aircraft, and his canteen cup leapt ten feet out in front of him, the hot coffee immediately freezing in a splatter pattern in the snow. In a matter of seconds his M-16 rifle, maintenance clipboard, and anything else not permanently affixed to his body, found a place in the snow.

As for Fegly, he was no more. By time I pulled off the mask to share in this joyous occasion with him, he was fifty yards back down from whence he came. I called to him, but due to either the deafness that comes with fear, or the squeaking and crunching of the snow, he did not hesitate, and continued what was surely to be a respectable Olympian record.

After catching my breath and scraping the frozen tears from my cheeks, I gathered my friend's belongings. I wiped the snow from them and thought of him. Of his shaking hands, his shifty, worried eyes. I thought of how he always worked so hard to do his job the best he could. I entertained the thought that he had brought this situation on himself by reading that horror book in the middle of a dark, Alaskan night. I sat examining myself, and my actions. I thought long and hard about how I had taken advantage of him and the situation.

Then I laughed my ass off, some more.

Fegly never spoke of the incident. He never told anyone the story of the attacking spawn of Satan, its piercing red eyes, and the horrific scream. When I returned to the tent with his equipment, explaining I found it on the trail, he gave no explanation. When the maintenance tent called to see why no one had come to fix the tires, he refused to answer the phone.

This particular sighting was never reported or investigated.

And humanity is better for it...

Hairy bushmen or Tornits were said to have occupied the Alaskan
frontier. Native Alaskans have many stories of their interactions.

THE PATROL

SOMEWHERE NEAR WALES, ALASKA,
in the Arctic Circle, circa 1983

I ENLISTED IN THE ARMY toward the end of the Cold War. It was a hasty decision, one made from sheer desperation—panic. I was working in Austin as a telephone cable installer. The company was a small outfit, and with it came a small budget, and even smaller minds, mainly, those of its managers. After about four months, I was getting the hang of things; that's always when they hit. In one week, I was laid off from my job, and, subsequently, dumped by my girlfriend. That seemed to be the course of things. The money goes away, and then the women. That was my belief, then. I wouldn't realize until later in life, she had plenty of other reasons to dump me; the money just facilitated an excuse.

About a week later, after a dozen, infertile job interviews, I found myself sitting in front of the Army recruiter. Papers on the desk, pen in hand. I remember looking at the contract.

Yellow and long. Too long to read. I signed it solely on the basis that so many others before me had done the same. Completely on uncorroborated, unsubstantiated, undeniable, historical fact. Millions had done it before me and survived.

I pressed pen to paper.

One week later I stood baldheaded in front of one of the loudest individuals I had ever heard. I got up earlier than I ever did in my whole life. Stood still longer than I ever did in my whole life. Yelled louder; ran farther; cleaned better; polished glossier; marched faster; and remained celibate longer. Thirteen weeks of my life dedicated to Army Basic Training, personal improvement, and learning about the mysteries of my fellow man.

A couple of weeks before graduation, our orders came in. After a particularly grueling physical training session, our drill instructor assembled the platoon in the gravel lot, in front of the company headquarters; three World War II era, white, wood-framed barracks. Sergeant Gray, an average-sized man, well toned by regular basic training workouts, and a face looking like it had been set ablaze then put out with a rake, took his regular place in front. He held his clipboard eye level then leafed with his thumb, fluttering the pages of the orders everyone had waited for these many weeks. He seemed to be getting some sort of gratification, sexual in nature, out of this prolonged presentation. Something, no doubt, he practiced many times. Some of the recruits had contracted assignments when they enlisted. They knew exactly where they were going. I, on the other hand, and many like me, signed up not for a duty location, but for a job. In my case, the infantry. This was another thing I found out later, the infantry was not necessarily a coveted technical field, or in very high demand in the free marketplace. But it sounded like fun at the time...

Hello?...

Anyway, Sergeant Gray started his pace, back and forth, explaining something about how he didn't feel it was right to read our assignments before we actually graduated, and that he didn't want to get our hopes up, or something like that. I don't know, I wasn't really listening. I was used to his here's-the-bone, snatch-it-away tactics. I just blocked him out until he finally, like every other time, capitulated, and started reading the names and their assignments.

I started thinking of faraway lands as he began his way down the alphabet. Anderson and Barker, to Douglas and Fullingcamp, and on and on he droned. Being raised in Texas, I had a fondness for the warmer climates. When I signed my enlistment papers, the recruiter explained I needed to fill in my dream sheet. This was a simple box at the bottom of the paperwork, divided into three rectangles. He told me it was very important and to choose the three places I would most like to be stationed, because the assignments officer would choose one of the three. This should have been my first clue. I picked Hawaii, Panama, and Italy. I thought of Italy, and how great it would be to be assigned in Europe, about the same time he called my name for a second time.

"Lawson! You fucking deaf?"

"No, Sergeant! Here, Sergeant!" I shouted.

"No, you're not deaf? Or yes, you're here?" he shouted.

"Correct, Sergeant," I answered. He didn't like that. That was one of his tactics to throw recruits off, make them confused. I caught on to this the second day behind the fence, and decided to try, at every encounter, to throw a little back his way. I usually got a few extra push-ups, but it did have its entertainment value.

You could tell he was now trying to catch up to the conversation. Had he asked if I was, or wasn't absent, or deaf, or here, or what?

"Maybe I'll just leave you for last, since you don't seem to know your name," was all he could come up with.

Now, later, it didn't matter to me. Knowing my assignment, or not knowing, wasn't going to get me there any faster. I remained silent.

He stared.

"Lawson!" he shouted again.

"Here, Sergeant," I repeated.

He looked down at his clipboard. "You and Logg get along okay?" he asked.

A surge of energy reddened my body. Logg was a full-blooded American Indian, straight off the reservation in South

Dakota. I hadn't really got to know him in the past few weeks, but he seemed okay. Quiet, and hard working. I also knew he was one of those who enlisted for a duty assignment: Hawaii. My breathing increased. I almost bellowed a triumphant yell. It took everything I had to hold it in. The yell would have been worth the pushups I would receive for losing my discipline.

Gray thumbed around in the papers a second or two longer. "Yeah, looks like you and Logg are going..." He paused. "Wait. No, Lawson, you're going to Alaska. Logg, you're going to Hawaii."

"No, no, no, that can't be right—" I stammered.

Sergeant Gray yanked the clipboard to his side. "You got something to say, Private?"

"Sergeant, Private Lawson requests permission to speak."

"Speak!"

"Could you check the list again, Sergeant? I requested Hawaii, Panama, or Italy," I said, as respectfully as I could.

"Holy shit, Lawson requested," he said, stepping a little closer to me. "Wake up, sweetheart, it's a new day. You're going to the land of the midnight sun—son. Pack an extra blanket."

I'm not sure if he said anything after that. I went back into my zone. Position of attention, heels together, back straight, eyes forward. I knew, deep down, he was messing with me. I waited until the end. Martinez, then Peterson. Thompson, then Williams.

Sergeant Gray dismissed the platoon. "You got 25 'til chow, ladies. Fall out!"

Bodies scrambled around me, running to make the barracks' showers first, and avoid the line. I remained in place.

Gray turned and made it halfway back to the headquarters building before he looked back and saw me. Tucking his clipboard under his arm, he quickly marched back to me. "What the fuck is your malfunction, Lawson?"

"Alaska?" I said, hoping he was just yanking my chain, and would look down and correct himself. Again.

"Alaska," he repeated. "Do you believe in God, Lawson?"

"Yes, Sergeant," I said; however, after this, I was having my doubts.

"Well, Lawson, God, in his wisdom, has used the United States Army to get you to Alaska. What you do with it is up to you. Carry on."

I executed a half-hearted about-face and started walking back to the barracks.

After a few steps, Sergeant Gray added, "Lawson."

I turned to look.

"You can do two years on your head. Get it done, then go someplace else. Hell, in twenty years, you could be right back here, squarin' some kids away, like me."

I think he meant this little bit of insight as motivation, but it just didn't seem to help me visualize my dreams. They definitely were not dreams of being a single, 40-year-old drill instructor, with a clipboard in Georgia.

Over the next two years, I became intimate with Alaska. Every bit of my time off, I spent outside. I hiked Denali State Park, snow skied Girdwood in the south, and snowmobiled the Brooks Range in the north. I scuba-dived the waters of Seward Bay, Prince William Sound, and Cook Inlet. I chiseled my way through three feet of ice, just to enter under it and explore the depths of Big Lake. I swam among whales, jellyfish, eels, and fur seals. I explored World War II gun emplacements that guarded the entrance to protected harbors and discovered the trash the soldiers threw in the waters below. I was chased by a bear near the base of Mount McKinley and by a moose abreast the Alaskan Range. In the dead of winter, I shared a C-ration pork meal with a hungry arctic fox near the Delta Junction. I was watched by eagles and owls, hidden from by ptarmigan and rabbit, and propositioned by the locals. In these two years, I traveled to Barrow, the farthest point north, to Kodiak in the south, Wales in the west, and well into the Yukon Territories to the east. I learned of Alaska, her nature, and her peoples. I loved her beauty, and kindness; her anger and despairs.

As for my job, I learned to love it also. I was an Arctic Infantry Parachutist, assigned to one of only three Airborne companies in Alaska. A scant 400 or so men. Most people go on vacation to go camping, pay someone to take them skydiving, spend money to go target practicing; God, and the United

States Army provided all these things for me, free of charge. Hell, they actually paid me to do them. They took me to the tundra in the winter and to the swamps in the summer. To the icy tops of the mountains and to the flowing streams in the valleys. From night blindness to snow blindness, and everywhere in between. They used the Airborne on every field problem, training exercise, or battle survey in Alaska. I deployed always.

One January, my platoon was sent north of Nome, to recon the tundra area near the Bering Sea. It was a common paranoia among the American military that the Alaskan coast was a vulnerability that must be protected. Born of this was a series of security measures involving air, sea, and land patrols. Unfortunately, I was in the latter.

Our platoon set up a base camp in a low-lying area, protected from the winds, about a mile from the Bering Sea. We had four ten-man tents to house thirty-eight of us. They were typical Army, round, pole tents, about seven feet tall. When we set them up, we lowered them to about three feet high. This allowed for maximum conservation of warmth but created very cramped living conditions.

Each of our squads took turns conducting day and nighttime patrols, not that anyone could tell the difference between the two. None of us had seen the sun since we left Anchorage. The only way you could tell day from night was by your watch, or by a faint attempt along the horizon for the sun to crest, yet refuse. We were briefed by our lieutenant, given grid coordinates, magnetic bearings, direction and distances, and 12 hours to complete the patrol. The actual distance we were assigned could easily be covered in 6 hours, but because of changing weather conditions or deep snow, they allotted double that time. The helicopters would pick us up around 6:00 pm and fly us to the start point. Most of the Seward Peninsula was exactly what you would think the Arctic would be. Flat and devoid of any prominent land markings. It seemed to roll on to the sea. This made for great practice in compass navigation and map orienteering; you had to completely rely on your compass. Over a six-hour movement, any slight deviation could take you miles off track, and if a whiteout came, the helicopters would never find you. That was bad in 40 below.

The weather had been kind to us. It was standard procedure to cease all operations at 70 below, but the temperature had remained in the 40 below range. There was practically no wind the three weeks we operated in the area, and after we started out on our patrols, the physical exertion warmed us up considerably. On the way, I noticed people starting to shed their heavy clothing. Stripping it off and hanging it someway to their body or rucksack. I had started the movement with my arctic mittens and parka, but both were now slung behind my neck. The night was an Alaskan night. Absolutely pitch dark. As we moved along in a Ranger file, I lost sight of the soldier just five yards in front of me. I wasn't worried; I just followed the trail they were leaving in the snow. I knew the guy behind me was doing the same.

At first, I found it strange, foolish actually, that a group of Americans, on foot, near the Bering Sea, were walking along in the dead of winter looking for something. After all, that's what a patrol is, you're out looking for something. With all the technology the United States had, it was odd they would elect to send soldiers out on foot to secure the Alaskan coastline. As I said, that's what I thought, at first. It wasn't until my second patrol that I understood. The Bering Sea in the dead of winter is a sheet of ice connecting North America to Siberia with some open channels of water created by strong ocean currents. If that wasn't scary enough, on my second patrol, we took helicopters to Tin City and witnessed what looked to be military parachute flares and green, Soviet gun tracer rounds being fired in Siberia, only 40 miles from our location. Apparently, the Soviets had the same idea. If an invasion were to occur, a simple plan would be to cross the frozen sea. Either country could invade by conducting a mass land movement assisted with navy transports. Granted it would have to be quick. The defending nation could simply bomb the ice and create impassible fractures. However, strategic ideas such as that took the fun out of this impending threat, so they continued these games. Twice, our lieutenant fired off a red star cluster in a half-hearted attempt at communication. And twice, they answered back with green flares.

We stopped trying to communicate.

On this night, we were making good time. Warm winds, the Chinook winds, coming up from the South Pacific, had apparently moved through this area in the past few weeks. You could always tell by the hard crust the snow developed, after it had been melted by these winds, and then quickly frozen again. Our snowshoes slid across this hard layer of snow, which made for easy travel. I was in my zone after about two hours. My eyes adjusted to the darkness, and I could make out silhouettes of land formations and sometimes of my fellow squad members. We stopped in a low area, and everyone adjusted their equipment and got some water. I took off my arctic trousers and put them in the rucksack. I was beginning to sweat a little, and that's the last thing you want to do in 40 below. You start sweating, and the moment you stop, you're in trouble. That water is going to freeze in a matter of seconds and you're a casualty. When we started off again, I remember how good I felt. I rolled my stocking cap up and exposed my face to the winter. We skidded along and I felt every bit of my body. My legs were hot, swollen with blood from the work, lungs tight, and shoulders numb from the weight of the pack. It wasn't long before my eyelashes started to collect ice and lengthen. It was a game we played sometimes, to see who could develop the longest lashes of ice. You could get yourself to the point where sight was impossible. Usually, I liked mine about a half inch long. That gave the world a rainbowed, halo effect I enjoyed. It provided something else to think about, other than the weight on your back, ache in your knees, or the next four hours walking in snowshoes. It made everything dreamlike.

After passing over a small rise, we descended in a Ranger file down into a short, narrow valley. It was there I first saw the burial mounds. I knew there was a lot of ancient occupation of Inuit people in this area. Later, I learned what I had seen was most likely remnants of the Birnirk culture, a prehistoric group that made small houses and hunted seal and caribou. The depressions in the area were probably dwelling foundations and for sure one large man-made mound. The valley was lined with small, scrubby pines these peoples probably used to build their houses. I looked up ahead and saw thirty or forty of these trees, not more than five or six feet tall in a cluster. The small ridge rise apparently protected them from the killing winds that normally swept everything off this land. They were so out of place, clumped up against the far side of the shallow draw. They were black as shadows on the snowy background, and I could make out their deformed shapes as they bent and twisted to the wind's command. These trees might have been hundreds of years old; the growing season for this latitude was probably only a few weeks a year. It would have taken many years, possibly centuries, for these trees to reach that height.

I looked back down at the footsteps left in the snow by the guy in front of me and tried to coax myself forward. The paratrooper walking behind me, not realizing I had stopped, bumped into my rucksack, then stepped around and continued down the trail. At this point, I got off the trail and walked to the curious clump of trees. They were maybe six feet tall and looked like they were in the shape of a thirty-or so-foot diameter ring. The cluster was a collection of both living and dead pines—some needleless and twisted, others nothing more than stumps. I worked my way through them and found myself standing at the base of a burial mound encircled by this bower. Here I realized the trees blocked the wind, and my environment became silent. I took in a deep breath and exhaled a fog.

I felt in my core that this place was something special. I walked the perimeter of the mound. Because of the layer of snow, I was unable to see any artifacts that may have been left there. Halfway around, I discovered a small pile of stones protruding through the ice.

Out of the corner of my eye, I saw a shimmer of light. I looked in its direction, but nothing was there.

I stopped, pulled off my left arctic mitten and reached down into my trouser cargo pocket. I retrieved a C-ration meal box and took out the main can: "Pork-Boned" (seriously, that's what it was called). I replaced it and searched my opposite pocket finding the tuna C-ration. In arctic tradition, I placed the can of tuna at the base of the mound, out of respect for the dead and for those who might have been left behind. I figured they would rather have tuna than pork-boned.

I saw the flash again. I reached up and scraped the icicle eyelashes I was growing and tried to clear my vision and then looked back down at the snow. That only enhanced the flashes. The light changed into colors of blues, greens, yellows, reds, and everything in between on the snow. There were beautiful waves of color crossing the landscape. It took me a few seconds, but then I realized what was happening. I looked up. Flowing far above our heads was the most spectacular light show I have ever seen. The northern lights, in all their glory, were painting the panorama. Waves of every color in the spectrum rolled across the sky. From horizon to horizon they spilled, reached, shot, and tickled. Fingers of red pointed across the blackness, wings of yellow flapped and soared toward the North Star, and blue waves rolled like calm surf back out to sea.

I looked back through the trees' twisted tentacles and could make out the dark silhouettes of the entire thirty-eight-man platoon, motionless against a bluish-white background. The entire line of men had stopped and were looking up at the lights. Half of them had already begun to dump their rucks in the snow, creating a place to sit and watch. Even though I was 30 yards from the nearest soldier, I heard them passing back from man to man the lieutenant's directive: "Chow time."

I turned back to the mound, dropped my shoulder strap, and dropped my ruck from my aching back. Digging out my parka, I wrapped it around me and butt-flopped into the snow, my back leaning against the mound. For the next hour, Alaska granted me something truly moving. Something I have never experienced since. Something I have never felt since. Something truly, only for me. I would see a green fish jumping through a yellow bug, horses running and eagles swooping. A train passed, then a whale. I pulled out the rest of my meal, and watched, and ate my food frozen; I didn't want to miss anything.

While sitting there, I thought about how these arctic people existed in such an unforgiving but miraculous place. I imagined the day of their death and how their family placed them here, under the frozen ground. How they would forever be facing skyward.

After about an hour, there seemed to be a sort of finale, and just before powers that be decided to fade, long bursts of reds flowered out.

Then it was gone.

I looked back and forth in the sky, hoping to catch another glimpse.

Nothing.

I waited about another ten minutes for an encore that never came. I heard something through the trees. I got up and walked through the circle. Then I heard the noise again: "Lawson!"

"Here!" I shouted back.

Sergeant Mills yelled, "Count off!"

Being at the back of the procession, I sounded off with "One!"

The trooper several yards in front of me repeated with "Two." And so on the count went until it reached the lieutenant. I went back and gathered my equipment, then joined my teammates once again. Our line of mankind stood in silent ovation as we waited to resume our patrol. I don't know if it was because this experience was so impactful or if we were just all too tired, but no one discussed what we saw. No comments of the experience. It wasn't discussed then, or to this very day. I think many of us understood its significance. Even when we returned to our base camp, nothing.

It was a private thing.

What can you say about beauty? Emerson once said, "Beauty without expression, tires. Things are pretty, graceful, rich, elegant, handsome, but until they speak to the imagination, not yet beautiful." It is something that can only be experienced, and to try to describe it diminishes it to nothing more than a black-and-white page.

Almost an insult.

I often contemplate the synchronicities in my life. The luck of being in the right place at the right time. The subtle draw to something unusual. The unlikely chance at discovering a sacred site in the vast blackness of the Arctic night. The unlikely coincidence of placing an offering as the skies burst to life.

I have never shared this story. During that long, frozen night, lying there with the dead, the land and the sky shared with me something irrepealable. To the best of my ability, I have now shared it with you.

From that night, I now know what beauty is.

I pray I shall never forget.

MY BROTHER'S KEEPER

LEAP CASTLE
Ireland, circa 2015

GOD IS A POWERFUL MOTIVATOR. His rules and those that interpret his rules are often the most powerful influences of people in a society. They influence the daily practices of the masses, government adherence or tolerance of civil discord, and of course—war.

Thaddeus was one such priest; a young man believed to be in the service of God. But also a man who had great ambition along with influence over his family and his surrounding clan. He, being the priest, was one of the only people in the area that had a public platform for spreading the word of God and his own ideology every Sabbath.

At the height of Thaddeus' influence, his world was in turmoil. His village and family castle were in a constant state of conflict and with the death of his father, Mulrooney

O'Carroll, the stability of the family was now in question. However, he was housed within a formidable fortress overlooking the lush green lands of Coolderry, Ireland. Behind these thick walls with strategically placed battlements, well-designed archer arrow slits, secret hatches and strong doors, Thaddeus was as safe as anyone could be in the 1500s. With one exception: he was the son of an O'Carroll, and the O'Carroll clan was one of the most ruthless in Ireland's history. Shortly after the death of his father, Thaddeus began a campaign to assume as his father's successor attempting to take control of the family and their homestead: Leap Castle.

I am ashamed to say, but I had never heard of Leap Castle, pronounced "lep," before my visit to Ireland in 2015. I had studied Irish lore and haunted places before we travelled, and while I was familiar with many haunted castles, fairy rings and forts, I completely missed Leap—one of the most haunted. So, when the group I was travelling with headed toward Leap Castle, I asked, what is Leap Castle? All of them stared at me like I was an idiot.

And I was...

I now know Leap Castle is one of the most haunted and spiritually active sites in Ireland. While there is some dispute of the actual start of the construction of the castle, most anyone involved in the estimation will say between the 12th and 15th centuries. Also, almost all would also agree that the location was the site of human occupation far longer than that. It is strategically placed on high ground and easily overlooks much of the surrounding lands. There is also evidence that druids once occupied the spot and performed ritualistic worship there, possibly involving sacrificial death.

Leap Castle was originally constructed by the O'Bannon clan and the castle was originally named *Leim Ui Bhanain*, which translates to "Leap of the O'Bannons." This was believed to be because the legend says there were two O'Bannon brothers that were vying for the position of family chieftain. It appears they had mutual respect for one another and devised a contest to determine which one would lead the family. They challenged themselves to leap from a high rock on the site of where the castle now stands, and the brother that survived would not only govern the clan but would also oversee the castle and its constructions. After they jumped, one did survive, and he assumed the role as chieftain. Other than any possible sacrifices conducted by the druids, this event began the blood-spattered history of Leap Castle.

When our group arrived, we were met by the castle's current owner, musician and gentleman, Sean Ryan. Sean and his wife, Anne, were gracious enough to open their doors to us and allow the group to explore their home. While Sean has conducted some restorations to the castle, he has done his best to keep it as authentic as possible, given that the castle was bombed by the IRA in 1920 and was almost completely destroyed by fire. In doing so, there are several locations within the structure that lend themselves to supporting many of the myths and legends about the building—mainly the chapel on the top floor and an oubliette behind one of its walls.

While chapels in general don't usually pique my interest, chapels on the top floor of a building with an oubliette do. An oubliette, modified from the French words "to forget," is basically a specific kind of dungeon. In the case of an oubliette, one with only one entrance in its ceiling, usually in the form of a locked hatch. Therefore, the Leap oubliette is a small shaft, at least three stories tall equipped with spikes in the bottom. In the 1800s the Darby family controlled the castle and during a renovation, three cartloads of human bones were removed from the oubliette. In some reported stories, hundreds of skeletons were disinterred from the walls. However, due to the size of what I saw, the story would be more accurate if written that hundreds of bones were recovered—I do not believe hundreds of bodies could have occupied that space, but over an 800-year period, what do I know?

Even then, this chapel, known now as The Bloody Chapel, was no doubt the scene of many murders. These

Thaddeus, the priest of Leap Castle was slain on the alter by his brother Teighe. His ghost is often seen in the castle's halls and in the Bloody Chapel.

murders were typically the killings of the O'Carroll's guests, usually people that had helped them with political influence or success in battle. They would invite them to a celebration at the castle, feast with them in the dining hall, then invite them up to celebrate mass. Once in the chapel and with the doors secured, armed men from an adjoining room would enter and the slaughter would begin. In one case, thirty-nine members of the MacMahon clan were murdered in their sleep, and possibly deposited in the oubliette. But the most famous of these killings would be that of our family priest, Thaddeus.

You see, in 1532, it is reported that Thaddeus was in the chapel celebrating the mysteries of the Eucharist with friends and family. He began the service before his brother Teighe arrived—this act was said to be a great insult to Teighe. Therefore, when Teighe arrived and saw the mass already underway, his anger exploded and he charged the sanctuary and thrust the blade of his sword through his brother, spilling Thaddeus' blood all over the altar.

That is where Thaddeus' spirit departed from his mortal body and that is where he is said to remain to this very day.

While there are many other stories of torture and murder in and around the castle, I would be remiss to exclude the famous Red Lady. Some of my traveling companions engaged themselves in trying to contact or locate this often-seen specter. Many previous visitors have reported seeing a woman in red holding a knife wandering the halls of the castle.

Mildred Darby lived in the castle in the late 1800s and reported a tall, dark woman wearing a scarlet silk dress who haunts the blue room. The blue room was previously known to be a child's nursery. Mildred said the Red Lady could be seen weeping at the foot of the children's beds.

Mildred's account would seem to support the history of the O'Carrolls' violent past. The legend is that the Red Lady was once a prisoner of the O'Carrolls. And with the O'Carrolls being cold-blooded murderers, it is not hard to imagine them being serial rapists as well. Although we do not know her name, it is believed she was held in a castle dungeon and kept for acts of sexual abuse and rape. The product of this violence was a baby of which when born, the O'Carrolls promptly killed. Stricken with inconsolable grief and a future of eternal abuse, she obtained a knife and killed herself—possibly the same knife used on the infant. It is believed her spirit roams the castle nightly, in search of the men that killed her child.

After my Bloody Chapel and oubliette exploration, I wandered the halls of Leap. I imagined the men and women that have walked these corridors for possibly 800 years. I imagined the love experienced here along with the fear and hatred. I observed the castle construction, spiral staircases and hidden arrow slits poised for an ambush. I saw the furniture and the rocks that are the bones and innards of this dwelling. However, I did not see the Red Lady, Thaddeus, or any of the other hundreds that were murdered or simply died on this land and within these walls.

I joined Sean and several others in the living room, and he played a few songs for us. It was a truly magical and happy occasion to be there with my friends and to witness this fine musician, in his incredible home, do what he truly loves.

After several hours we found ourselves taking final pictures, passing handshakes and hugs, then walking reluctantly up the driveway and back to the road, all the while Sean and Anne waving goodbye. Lynn and I stopped with our friend Sharon Leong just before we got out of the view of the castle and took one last picture. Then that was it, another check off of my bucket list that I didn't even know I had.

It was several weeks later while reminiscing about this adventure that I saw it. Going through the photos on my phone and posts from friends on Facebook. Then, there it was, the photo taken by Sharon. That last photo of the castle. The powerful rock façade. Sean and Anne at the front door. The blue sky. And the image of a priest standing in the second story window just above the front door, looking down at us.

No shit.

I have the picture.

THE SPIRITS

LANTAU ISLAND,
Hong Kong, circa 1992

UNDER THE COVER OF DARKNESS, we had slipped the USS *Nimitz* aircraft carrier up the East Lamma Channel, between George Island and Ap Lei Chau Island then rounded Green Island to finally drop anchor near the mouth of Victoria Harbour, Hong Kong. When morning came, the occupants of that city were surprised with an aircraft carrier just offshore and six thousand sailors coming to town with a month's paycheck in each wallet—assuming they had not spent it on junk food or lost it gambling on the way. This was my second shore excursion on this British Territory and one of my favorite destinations—friendly people, inexpensive beer, and no shortage of places to go and things to do.

Something I learned early on while traveling in Asian countries: people do not like talking about the paranormal. It seems to me, many believe the more you talk about it, the more likely you will fall victim to it. The most information I received from the local people I was able to speak with was in Hong Kong. Probably because of the extended British occupation and the necessity of the people of Hong Kong to learn English.

In my normal fashion, with a little research in the *Nimitz* library, (yep, it has a library), I had already planned my destination and arranged my shore liberty for the entire four days in port; another sailor had charged me seventy dollars for him to cover the day of my duty-watch and it was worth it.

In my readings on Chinese myths and legends, there were two specifically that intrigued me. One was the Shui Gui. The Shui Gui, or Souls of the Drowned, are literally the spirits of people who have drowned and are waiting for living humans to come near the place they drowned so the Shui Gui can drown them as well. Since at that point in my life I had experienced two near drowning incidents, the Shui Gui caught my attention. A legend such as this would have wide acceptance on Lake Travis, where I currently patrol and conduct underwater recoveries. Many of the drownings at Lake Travis occur at the same places where previous drownings have taken place, leading to the belief there is something more at work here.

The other was the Hungry Ghosts. These spirits, because of their selfish and cruel behavior in life are doomed to waste away in the underworld. And like most other cultures, some Chinese have the belief that departed souls, whether in the form of ghost or wraiths, return from the dead to haunt a certain location, complete some unfinished task, or terrorize the living. Some Chinese believe in demons and other spiritual entities that have never been human and that influence or exercise power over people. Then there are the mythical monsters that serve both good and evil purposes. As you can see, westerners have quite a bit in common with easterners.

I made my way off the gangplank and into the throng of the mass exodus of the ship. Soon I found myself stepping off a ferry and onto a commercial pier in Victoria City. After a brief check by their customs authority and navigating my way through the sailors, police, and prostitutes, I was at a booth along Belcher Bay, buying a jetfoil ferry ticket to my destination goal: Lantau Island.

The jetfoil ticket was a little more expensive, but I had never ridden on one, so I decided to go for it. It was completely worth it. The boat was fast and rose above the choppy waves giving an incredibly smooth ride.

Lantau Island was actually my second choice; my first choice was a former British military officers' barracks named the Murray House, located in Central Hong Kong, a business district in the heart of the city. I was incredibly excited about this very historic and haunted location. It was reported that during World War II the Japanese had occupied Murray House for almost four years. During this occupation, it was reported that the Japanese used the location as a detention center and reportedly tortured and murdered many prisoners there. Some prisoners were reported to have committed suicide rather than face the Japanese torture techniques. In the twenty years after the war, countless sightings, strange experiences, and unexplainable sounds were reported by the government workers assigned to the offices within the structure. So much that in the early 1960s, government workers requested and received approval for the Murray House to be cleansed through the means of exorcism. On May 19, 1963, ninety Buddhist monks gathered at the Murray House for ten hours and conducted the exorcism ceremony. During the ritual, a list of names of those known to have died through the atrocities committed there were written onto tablets and before midnight taken outside and burned.

But the more I researched, the more I learned. An additional exorcism was conducted in 1974 that was actually televised. Then, unfortunately in 1982, the Murray House was dismantled, block by block, and stored. It wasn't until 2017 that I resurrected my fascination with the Murray House and learned that in 2001, the Chinese government rebuilt the Murray House in Stanley, a city south of Victoria. It now serves as a shopping destination.

As my second choice, Lantau Island is the home to three things I was interested in: Po Lin Buddhist Monastery, the Shaolin Wushu Martial Arts Center, and Fan Lau Fort, an outpost to combat piracy in the early 1700s.

As we approached the island, I was surprised to see how mountainous it was. While there were a lot of signs of human occupation, houses, businesses, and roads, the entire island seemed to be covered in lush vegetation. Once off the pier, I grabbed the bus to the monastery. Other than a British couple, I was the only westerner on the bus, and no one would sit next to me. This made the trip a little disturbing and sort of comfortable all at the same time. But the drive was gorgeous, with beautiful flowers and strange birds everywhere.

Once at the monastery I signed in and took the general tour. I was disappointed to find out the monastery was founded only in the early 1900s; however, the architecture was interesting, and I was able to see the sculptures of the three Buddhas, past, present, and future. The part most interesting was that the monastery had recently started construction of what they would be able to boast as the largest Buddha in the world—a complete contradiction of Buddhist dogma...But, great for tourism.

After the tour, it was early afternoon and I got a bus heading for Tai O Fishing Village and the Shaolin Wushu Cultural Center. While the landscape was amazing, the bus ride was horrific. My experience was bloated with bad roads, smelly occupants, and a bit car "bus" sick. Dusk was upon us as we arrived, and I grabbed the first motel I came to and went straight to sleep.

The following morning, I hired a taxi and arrived at the Shaolin Center before 7:00 am. I wanted to make sure I arrived early and did not have to rush. Sadly, when I went to check in, I realized the school started at 5:00 am.

I should have known...

For the next three days, five hours each day, I endured an introduction to Shaolin Kung-fu. Being a martial artist and having a black belt in Tae Kwon Do, I thought it would be relatively easy. I was wrong. I knew nothing compared to these masters who not only studied the art but also lived the philosophy.

I was assigned to a monk who was not only a teacher but a tour guide as well. Over the next three days, 5:00 am to 11:00 am, we became friends; however, I never had more bruises on my body in my entire life. We began with animal forms on the first day, the tiger, dragon, and crane, and continued them along with intense power and stretching exercises. To spiritual Chinese people, most animals are symbolic of something in their life. Each can mean something important. The tiger symbolizes power and energy, the dragon is strength and good luck, and the crane longevity and peace.

The odd thing was, while the physical demands of Kung Fu are challenging, it was the meditation that I found most difficult. The search for the "Spirit." Forcing my mind to be clear of all thought, devoid of any internal dialogue, yet at the same time being aware of every sense and everything around me was impossible for me to attain in such a short time. The deep level of understanding and lucidity of the mind is impossible for some to accomplish in a lifetime. This intimate experience gave me a sense of clarity that I feel is a key for true paranormal investigators. It gave me a way to reach out, without relying on gadgetry, and truly listen and feel the world around me. I didn't really know what to expect from the center; however, I was not disappointed.

That afternoon I left the center to explore on my own and research the area for any weirdness. While there were many people to speak with, they were mainly interested in US currency, not sharing credible information about local legends or hauntings. The one subject that did reoccur with the people I met was that of the hungry ghosts. Everyone basically expressed these are the spirits of people who did something wrong or behaved badly when they were living. I also got the impression that many Chinese did not like the word "ghost," but more often referred to the departed as their ancestors. This led up to them telling me about the Hungry Ghost Festival every August. Essentially, what I gathered from what I was told, this festival is a Chinese

Halloween for adults—a very simplistic view, I know, but probably pretty accurate.

One old woman operating a small shop was very helpful. She had lived through the Japanese occupation and had fled from village to village to stay away from the soldiers, who I believe she said ate people—seriously. She spoke very broken English but that seemed to be what she said. However, she did like Americans very much.

I spent several hours talking with her. She asked what I was doing on the island and asked about my plans. I told her I had visited the monastery, the Shaolin Center, and tomorrow I had plans to see Fan Lau Fort. Immediately, she stopped and asked why. I explained to her that I visit battlefields and forts for a hobby. Once again, she asked me why. I tried to explain that many of the men that influenced my life served in some branch of the military and it was kind of my way to keep those warriors' memories alive. She said I should not go to the fort. I asked why. I tried to get her to be specific; however, all I could get from her was that it was not a good place and that nothing good ever happened there. She told me that pirates lived there, and many died there. This supported a little of what I had read about the fort. There was about a ten-year period where a group of pirates took over and occupied the fort, but it was retaken thereafter. She said that many years ago she had gone by the fort and she knew it was a bad place. I told her I needed to go and that I was sure everything would be all right. With that said, in the next fifteen minutes the old woman equipped me with everything I needed for my visit to Fan Lau Fort: a cloth package of cooked rice, a lighter, a lotus candle, three plastic bowls, three kinds of beans, and a stack of paper play money. It only cost me $17.00. Probably a day's wage for her. I gave her a twenty-dollar bill, which she conveniently stowed away, and I never saw the $3.00 in change...

We said our goodbyes and I continued my village exploration until dark.

The following morning, I was at the Shaolin Center on time. I sufficiently exerted myself attempting to perform in the way my body was never intended. Then I finally found myself in the back of a clean, semi-new taxi heading to Fan Lau Fort. By map it was only a few miles away, but by road it took us what seemed to be an hour to travel—maybe ten miles. When we arrived, there was no one in the vicinity. Either because it was the off-season for tourists or because it was in the middle of the week, I didn't know.

As we neared the fort, there was a large construction area along the roadway that appeared to be new apartments of some kind. They appeared finished; however, they were not occupied and looked to be falling into disrepair. The taxi driver pulled off the shoulder of the road and stopped.

He said, "Fan Lau."

I asked for the visitor center.

He pointed to a trail off into the brush; a wooden sign with Chinese markings stood to one side. He pointed to the trail. "Fan Lau."

I was not about to get robbed or murdered on this island. I stared at him in the rearview mirror.

He opened his door and got out. He motioned for me to do the same. I grabbed my backpack and got out. He motioned for me to follow him down the trail and I did. It wound back and forth through the undergrowth until we came over a small rise. There, the trail straightened and led down to the square, walled fort with the remnants of several other attached spaces. What remained of the fort were nothing more than a series of walls and some foundation. But as described, it overlooked the southern point of Lantau Island at a height of about 400 feet above the sea.

At this point I tried to tell the taxi driver I would be spending the rest of the day here and that he could go. Once he understood, he made me understand that there would be no way for me to get back, because there are no other taxis in the area. We did some humorous though highly unintelligible negotiations and it seemed we agreed on him staying the rest of the day for $40.00.

After we agreed, he went back to the taxi and I assumed took a nap. I, on the other hand, explored the ruins. It was obvious that the site had been looted by the locals over the past hundred years. Any roofing material, wood, and much of the rocks used to construct the walls were gone. The government had obviously come in and cut away the surrounding vegetation but done little else. Within the walls there was not much to see so I did two widening circles of the perimeter of the fort. Anyone with the understanding of warfare could see why this location was selected for the fort. With suppressing the threat of piracy its number one priority, this fort was positioned in such a way as to see the approach of any ship for miles. However, due to the fort's placement on the hill, and being relatively small, it would have been of little use if several ships decided to lay siege. There were several trails leading away from the fort that seemed to all weave themselves around and back up to the roadway.

I sat down and surveyed the site. It was picturesque, luscious green vegetation, a calm blue sea, and birdsongs all around me. I decided to walk contours on both sides of the crumbling fort. I was searching for anything unusual, and of course where there was human occupation, there would be graves somewhere. After close to two hours of walking back and forth I found two depressions that appeared to be the approximate size for a human body, but nothing else, other than a little blue, almost black, magpie that followed and watched me. There were no human markings, signs, or anything else of immediate interest. I wished I had brought a metal detector with me.

I was disappointed with the lack of physical evidence of some battle or death here. On the surface, the fort just seemed to be nothing more than the fragments of an old building. My intuition was telling me more. I have been to many famously haunted places. Places that have a legitimate claim to the paranormal, and I have felt nothing. Fan Lau Fort was not one of these places. There was no Woman in White story, no details of a heinous murder or horrendous torture, no tombstone marking a mass grave. But I felt something.

Something was there at Fan Lau Fort.

I headed back to the interior of the fort and sat on the southernmost wall. I decided to practice what I was learning at the Shaolin Center and dropped my backpack. I sat down and tried to clear my mind. The little bird landed on the rocks near me. I had some sort of crackers in my backpack, so I dug them out and broke off a piece and then threw it near the bird—he was not interested. He jumped to another rock. I relaxed and I tried to push all my responsibilities away. I closed my eyes and tried to get the *Nimitz* out of my mind. Home out of my mind. Traffic, ferries, aircraft, taxis, money, time— all out of my mind. I tried to listen to the land. I tried to listen to my gut. I tried to hear with my feelings. To reach out to someone, anyone, that may be there.

Maybe an hour went by when I got an overwhelming feeling that I was being watched. I opened my eyes and the

Sometimes bluish-green or even black, the Qingniao are birds of the Orient that bear important messages from the goddess, Queen Mother of the West.

bird was now on the ground, hopping around. Everything else was the same.

Everyone has had the feeling of being watched. Many people have talked with me about it. The feeling that someone or something is staring at you. I had been paranoid before, thinking that someone *could* be watching me, but this feeling was different. This feeling was not something voluntary. Not something pleasant. Like the old woman had said, nothing good ever happened here.

I got to my feet; it was difficult because part of my legs and feet had fallen asleep. I may have fallen asleep during my meditation as well. The sun was still just above the horizon but was falling fast. I decided to head back, but then I remembered the hungry ghosts. I opened my backpack and took out my offering: a cloth package of cooked rice, a lotus candle, a lighter, three plastic bowls, three kinds of beans, and a stack of paper play money. The bird jumped up on the wall and watched. I sat the bag of rice on a flat stone nearest the southwest corner of the fort's wall. Placed the three bowls beside it along with the play money. I heard footsteps behind me and looked back—it was my taxi driver walking across the interior yard down to me. He looked perplexed as he watched what I was doing. I smiled at him and continued. I opened the first package of beans and started to pour them into one of the bowls. The driver made a sound, and I saw he was shaking his head. He squatted down next to me. I don't know what he was thinking as to why I was performing this ritual. Whether I had a loved one recently die, or I was trying to appease the dead. In any case, he motioned that he would show me, then he pointed up to the bird and smiled. He said a word, I assumed was the name of the kind of bird and then handed me back the cloth of rice and the three bowls. He pointed at the lighter and then the candle. I lit the candle. He motioned that I use both hands and place the rice on one side of the candle. Then with both hands place a bowl down. He showed me how to pour the beans into my hand from the bag, then using both hands pour them into the bowl. Then again with the other beans, then again with the last beans, lentils, I think. The candle was now surrounded, north, south, east, and west with edible offerings. Finally, he motioned for the money. I repeated their placement as before, with both hands. He knelt down next to me and waited for me to get into that same position. I did. He leaned forward and closed his eyes.

So did I.

I don't know what he was thinking, or what I was supposed to think. But while we knelt there, the fear went away. Paranoia went away. It was like a bubble formed around us. I felt compassion for those sailors that approached these shores, for those soldiers assigned as the watchers of the fort, and for the dead that may have spent their last moments on this same soil, staring and seeing this same sky for the last time as everything faded.

As sound faded.

After many minutes, my taxi driver rose to his feet and I joined him. We walked silently to the car and the bird followed. I last saw him sitting on a branch as we drove away.

I fell asleep on the way back to the motel.

Years later, after doing some research on Chinese folklore, I found out that blue or green birds, the Qingniao, were the special messengers of the Queen Mother. My little bird may have simply liked tourists, he may have been protecting his nest, or he may have followed me for other reasons. Now that twenty-five years separates me from who I was then, I wish I would have been more attentive to that one and only thing at Fan Lau Fort that seemed to want my attention.

The problem with being a paranormalist is that there is never enough time. The tiny signs or fleeting experiences are in the actions and situations you are not necessarily looking for or expect. Most times they are impossible to document. Impossible to qualify. Often times, impossible to explain. What I do know is that we do not have to travel around the world to find these signs or have these experiences.

The spirit is everywhere.

The dead are everywhere.

They are in your town.

All you have to do is look.